LIVERPOOL FC
CHAMPIONS
OF EUROPE

LIVERPOOL FC ANNUAL SPECIAL EDITION

Written by Mark Platt
Designed by Chris Dalrymple

g

A Grange Publication

ISBN 9781913034429

CONTENTS

EUROPEAN ROYALTY

After defeating Tottenham Hotspur to win the 2019 Champions League, Liverpool are now outright third on the European Cup winning roll honour with six triumphs. Only two other teams have won more...

13 - REAL MADRID
(1956, 1957, 1958, 1959, 1960, 1966, 1998, 2000, 2002, 2014, 2016, 2017, 2018)

7 - AC MILAN
(1963, 1969, 1989, 1990, 1994, 2003, 2007)

6 - LIVERPOOL
(1977, 1978, 1981, 1984, 2005, 2019)

5 - BAYERN MUNICH   BARCELONA
(1974, 1975, 1976, 2001, 2013)   (1992, 2006, 2009, 2011, 2015)

4 - AJAX
(1971, 1972, 1973, 1995)

3 - INTERNAZIONALE   MANCHESTER UNITED
(1964, 1965, 2010)   (1968, 1999, 2008)

2 - BENFICA (1961, 1962)   **NOTTINGHAM FOREST** (1979, 1980)
JUVENTUS (1985, 1996)   **PORTO** (1987, 2004)

1 - CELTIC (1967) **FEYENOORD** (1970) **ASTON VILLA** (1982) **HAMBURG** (1983)
STEAUA BUCHAREST (1986) **PSV EINDHOVEN** (1988) **RED STAR BELGRADE** (1991)
MARSEILLE (1993) **BORUSSIA DORTMUND** (1997) **CHELSEA** (2012)

INTRODUCTION

2019 will forever be remembered as the year Liverpool Football Club firmly cemented itself as part of European royalty.

For the sixth time in the club's history they were crowned as the undisputed Kings of the continent.

Victory over Tottenham Hotspur on an unforgettable night in Madrid secured the most coveted prize in club football.

It was a momentous triumph. One that reverberated around the globe.

After narrowly missing out on lifting the Champions League trophy the season before, the Reds bounced back in style to banish the pain of that defeat to Real Madrid in Kiev.

It wasn't all plain sailing in 2018/19 though.

Three away defeats in the group phase meant progress to the knockout rounds hung in the balance prior to a priceless home win against Napoli.

That paved the way for a mouth-watering two-legged tie with German giants Bayern Munich. Following a goalless draw at Anfield the Reds were being written off but an outstanding performance in Bavaria sent out an ominous warning to their rivals.

Although Porto were comfortably disposed of in the quarter-final, Liverpool were considered the underdogs going into an eagerly anticipated last four clash with Barcelona.

A crushing 3-0 defeat in the Nou Camp belied the nature of the game but left Klopp's team on the brink of elimination.

What followed defied belief and left the press searching for new superlatives as Anfield's greatest-ever comeback unfolded. Amid a raucous atmosphere, Liverpool turned the tie completely on its head to run out 4-3 aggregate winners and memorably clinch a place in the final.

All roads then led to the Spanish capital for a historic all-English encounter with Tottenham Hotspur and a famous night at the Estadio Metropolitano.

It got off to the perfect start when Mo Salah scored from the penalty spot inside the opening minutes. However, a nervous wait ensued until Divock Origi's late strike sealed victory and sparked wild celebrations.

14 years since their last success in the competition, Liverpool were Champions of Europe once again.

The following day, over 750,000 people flooded the streets of Merseyside to hail their heroes.

Jürgen Klopp and his players had written their names indelibly into Liverpool legend.

It had been a remarkable journey. One that Liverpudlians will never tire of reliving. This is the story of how it was achieved…

WE'VE CONQUERED ALL OF EUROPE...

We're Never Gonna Stop
From Paris Down To Turkey
We've Won The Lot
Bob Paisley and Bill Shankly
The Fields of Anfield Road
We Are Loyal Supporters
And We Come From Liverpool
Allez Allez Allez
Allez Allez Allez
Allez Allez Allez
Allez Allez Allez

Anfield

ANFIELD HOME FIXTURES

Liverpool v PSG,
CL Group Phase, 18.9.2018

Liverpool v Red Star Belgrade,
CL Group Phase, 24.10.2018

Liverpool v Napoli,
CL Group Phase, 11.12.2018

Liverpool v Bayern Munich,
CL Round of 16, 1st leg, 19.2.2019

Liverpool v Porto,
CL Quarter-final, 1st leg, 9.4.2019

Liverpool v Barcelona,
CL Semi-final, 2nd leg, 7.5.2019

London 1978: Liverpool v
Club Brugge 10.5.78

Paris 1981: Liverpool v
Real Madrid 27.5.81

Paris: PSG v Liverpool,
CL Group Phase, 28.11.2018

Barcelona: Barcelona v Liverpool,
CL Semi-final first leg, 1.5.2019

Porto: Porto v Liverpool,
CL Quarter-final, 2nd leg, 17.4.2019

Madrid 2019: Liverpool v
Tottenham Hotspur 1.6.19

In their quest to win a sixth European crown, Liverpool visited six different countries during the course of the 2018/19 Champions League campaign, clocking up almost 13,000 air miles in the process. From Naples to Madrid, via Belgrade, Paris, Munich, Porto and Barcelona, it was an emotional roller-coaster journey that contained many highs but also a few lows – a crusade that is now part of history and one that will forever rank alongside the unforgettable runs to European glory in '77, '78, '81, '84 and '05.

 European Cup

 This Season's Games

 Munich: Bayern v Liverpool, CL Round of 16, 2nd leg, 13.3.2019

 Belgrade: Red Star Belgrade v Liverpool, CL Group Phase, 6.11.2018

 Rome 1977: Liverpool v Borussia Moenchengladbach 25.5.77
Rome 1984: Liverpool v AS Roma 30.5.84

 Istanbul 2005: Liverpool v AC Milan 25.5.05

 Naples: Napoli v Liverpool, CL Group Phase, 3.10.2018

Liverpool Football Club's complete record in the European Cup/Champions League 1964 to 2019

1964//65

Preliminary round

1st leg	17.8.64	KR Reykjavik	(a)	5-0
2nd leg	14.9.64	KR Reykjavik	(h)	6-1

Aggregate score: 11-1

First round

1st leg	25.11.64	Anderlecht	(h)	3-0
2nd leg	16.12.64	Anderlecht	(a)	1-0

Aggregate score: 4-0

Quarter-final

1st leg	10.2.65	Cologne	(a)	0-0
2nd leg	17.3.65	Cologne	(h)	0-0

Aggregate score: 0-0

Play-off	24.3.65	Cologne	(n)	2-2

Liverpool win on toss of a disc

Semi-final

1st leg	4.5.65	Inter Milan	(h)	3-1
2nd leg	12.5.65	Inter Milan	(a)	0-3

Aggregate score: 3-4

1966/67

First round

1st leg	28.9.66	Petrolul Ploiesti	(h)	2-0
2nd leg	12.10.66	Petrolul Ploiesti	(a)	1-3

Aggregate score: 3-3

Play-off	19.10.66	Petrolul Ploiesti	(n)	2-0

Second round

1st leg	7.12.66	Ajax	(a)	1-5
2nd leg	14.12.66	Ajax	(h)	2-2

Aggregate score: 3-7

1973/74

First round

1st leg	19.9.73	Jeunesse d'Esch	(a)	1-1
2nd leg	3.10.73	Jeunesse d'Esch	(h)	2-0

Aggregate score: 3-1

Second round

1st leg	24.10.73	Red Star Belgrade	(a)	1-2
2nd leg	6.11.73	Red Star Belgrade	(h)	1-2

Aggregate score: 2-4

1976/77

First round

1st leg	14.9.76	Crusaders	(h)	2-0
2nd leg	28.9.76	Crusaders	(a)	5-0

Aggregate score: 7-0

Second round

1st leg	20.10.76	Trabzonspor	(a)	0-1
2nd leg	3.11.76	Trabzonspor	(h)	3-0

Aggregate score: 3-1

Quarter-final

1st leg	2.3.77	Saint-Etienne	(a)	0-1
2nd leg	16.3.77	Saint-Etienne	(h)	3-1

Aggregate score: 3-2

Semi-final

1st leg	6.4.77	FC Zurich	(a)	3-1
2nd leg	20.4.77	FC Zurich	(h)	3-0

Aggregate score: 6-1

Final (Rome)

	25.5.77	Borussia M'gladbach	3-1

1977/78

First round

(Liverpool received a bye)

Second round

1st leg	19.10.77	Dynamo Dresden	(h)	5-1
2nd leg	2.11.77	Dynamo Dresden	(a)	1-2

Aggregate score: 6-3

Quarter-final

1st leg	1.3.78	Benfica	(a)	2-1
2nd leg	15.3.78	Benfica	(h)	4-1

Aggregate score: 6-2

Semi-final

1st leg	29.3.78	Borussia M'gladbach	(a)	1-2
2nd leg	12.4.78	Borussia M'gladbach	(h)	3-0

Aggregate score: 4-2

Final (Wembley)

	10.5.78	Club Brugge	1-0

1978/79

First round

1st leg	13.9.78	Nottingham Forest	(a)	0-2
2nd leg	27.9.78	Nottingham Forest	(h)	0-0

Aggregate score: 0-2

1979/80

First round

1st leg	19.9.79	Dinamo Tbilisi	(h)	2-1
2nd leg	3.10.79	Dinamo Tbilisi	(a)	0-3

Aggregate score: 2-4

1980/81

First round

1st leg	17.9.80	Oulu Palloseura	(a)	1-1
2nd leg	1.10.80	Oulu Palloseura	(h)	10-1

Aggregate score: 11-2

Second round

1st leg	22.10.80	Aberdeen	(a)	1-0
2nd leg	5.11.80	Aberdeen	(h)	4-0

Aggregate score: 5-0

Quarter-final

1st leg	4.3.81	CSKA Sofia	(h)	5-1
2nd leg	18.3.81	CSKA Sofia	(a)	1-0

Aggregate score: 6-1

Semi-final

1st leg	8.4.81	Bayern Munich	(h)	0-0
2nd leg	22.4.81	Bayern Munich	(a)	1-1

Aggregate score: 1-1 (Liverpool win on away goals)

Final (Paris)

	27.5.81	Real Madrid		1-0

1981/82

First round

1st leg	16.9.81	Oulu Palloseura	(a)	1-0
2nd leg	30.9.81	Oulu Palloseura	(h)	7-0

Aggregate score: 8-0

Second round

1st leg	21.10.81	AZ67 Alkmaar	(a)	2-2
2nd leg	4.11.81	AZ67 Alkmaar	(h)	3-2

Aggregate score: 5-4

Quarter-final

1st leg	3.3.82	CSKA Sofia	(h)	1-0
2nd leg	17.3.82	CSKA Sofia	(a)	0-2

Aggregate score: 1-2

1982/83

First round

1st leg	14.9.82	Dundalk	(a)	4-1
2nd leg	28.9.82	Dundalk	(h)	1-0

Aggregate score: 5-1

Second round

1st leg	19.10.82	HJK Helsinki	(a)	0-1
2nd leg	2.11.82	HJK Helsinki	(h)	5-0

Aggregate Score: 5-1

Quarter-final

1st leg	2.3.83	Widzew Lodz	(a)	0-2
2nd leg	16.2.83	Widzew Lodz	(h)	3-2

Aggregate score: 3-4

1983/84

First round

1st leg	14.9.83	Odense BK	(a)	1-0
2nd leg	28.9.83	Odense BK	(h)	5-0

Aggregate score: 6-0

Second round

1st leg	19.10.83	Athletic Bilbao	(h)	0-0
2nd leg	2.11.83	Athletic Bilbao	(a)	1-0

Aggregate score: 1-0

Quarter-final

1st leg	7.3.84	Benfica	(h)	1-0
2nd leg	21.3.84	Benfica	(a)	4-1

Aggregate score: 5-1

Semi-final

1st leg	11.4.84	Dinamo Bucharest	(h)	1-0
2nd leg	25.4.84	Dinamo Bucharest	(a)	2-1

Aggregate score: 3-1

Final (Rome)

	30.5.84	AS Roma		1-1

(Liverpool win 4-2 on pens)

1984/85

First round

1st leg	19.9.84	Lech Poznan	(a)	1-0
2nd leg	3.10.84	Lech Poznan	(h)	4-0

Aggregate score: 5-0

Second round

1st leg	24.10.84	Benfica	(h)	3-1
2nd leg	7.11.84	Benfica	(a)	0-1

Aggregate score: 3-2

Quarter-final

1st leg	6.3.85	Austria Vienna	(a)	1-1
2nd leg	20.3.85	Austria Vienna	(h)	4-1

Aggregate score: 5-2

Semi-final

1st leg	10.4.85	Panathinaikos	(h)	4-0
2nd leg	24.4.85	Panathinaikos	(a)	1-0

Aggregate score: 5-0

Final (Brussels)

	29.5.85	Juventus		0-1

2001/02

Qualifying round

1st leg	8.8.01	Haka	(a)	5-0
2nd leg	21.8.01	Haka	(h)	4-1

Aggregate score: 9-1

First Group phase

	11.9.01	Boavista	(h)	1-1
	19.9.01	Borussia Dortmund	(a)	0-0
	26.9.01	Dynamo Kiev	(h)	1-0
	16.10.01	Dynamo Kiev	(a)	2-1
	24.10.01	Boavista	(a)	1-1
	30.10.01	Borussia Dortmund	(h)	2-0

Second Group phase

	20.11.01	Barcelona	(h)	1-3
	5.12.01	AS Roma	(a)	0-0
	20.2.02	Galatasaray	(h)	0-0
	26.2.02	Galatasaray	(a)	1-1
	13.3.02	Barcelona	(a)	0-0
	19.3.02	AS Roma	(h)	2-0

Quarter-final

1st leg	3.4.02	Bayer Leverkusen	(h)	1-0
2nd leg	9.4.02	Bayer Leverkusen	(a)	2-4

Aggregate score: 3-4

2002/03

First group phase

	Date	Opponent		Score
	17.9.02	Valencia	(a)	0-2
	25.9.02	Basel	(h)	1-1
	2.10.02	Spartak Moscow	(h)	5-0
	22.10.02	Spartak Moscow	(a)	3-1
	30.10.02	Valencia	(h)	0-1
	12.11.02	Basel	(a)	3-3

2004/05

Qualifying round

	Date	Opponent		Score
1st leg	10.8.04	Grazer AK	(a)	2-0
2nd leg	24.8.04	Grazer AK	(h)	0-1

Aggregate score: 2-1

Group phase

	Date	Opponent		Score
	15.9.04	Monaco	(h)	2-0
	28.9.04	Olympiacos	(a)	0-1
	19.10.04	Deportivo La Coruna	(h)	0-0
	3.11.04	Deportivo La Coruna	(a)	1-0
	23.11.04	Monaco	(a)	0-1
	8.12.04	Olympiacos	(h)	3-1

First knockout round

	Date	Opponent		Score
1st leg	22.2.05	Bayer Leverkusen	(h)	3-1
2nd leg	9.3.05	Bayer Leverkusen	(a)	3-1

Aggregate score: 6-2

Quarter-final

	Date	Opponent		Score
1st leg	5.4.05	Juventus	(h)	2-1
2nd leg	13.4.05	Juventus	(a)	0-0

Aggregate score: 2-1

Semi-final

	Date	Opponent		Score
1st leg	27.4.05	Chelsea	(a)	0-0
2nd leg	3.5.05	Chelsea	(h)	1-0

Aggregate score: 1-0

Final (Istanbul)

	Date	Opponent		Score
	25.5.05	AC Milan		3-3

Liverpool win 3-2 on pens

2005/06

First qualifying round

	Date	Opponent		Score
1st leg	13.7.05	TNS	(h)	3-0
2nd leg	19.7.05	TNS	(a)	3-0

Aggregate score: 6-0

Second qualifying round

	Date	Opponent		Score
1st leg	26.7.05	FBK Kaunas	(a)	3-1
2nd leg	2.8.05	FBK Kaunas	(h)	2-0

Aggregate score: 5-1

Third qualifying round

	Date	Opponent		Score
1st leg	10.8.05	CSKA Sofia	(a)	3-1
2nd leg	23.8.05	CSKA Sofia	(h)	0-1

Aggregate score: 3-2

Group phase

	Date	Opponent		Score
	13.9.05	Real Betis	(a)	2-1
	28.9.05	Chelsea	(h)	0-0
	19.10.05	Anderlecht	(a)	1-0
	1.11.05	Anderlecht	(h)	3-0
	23.11.05	Real Betis	(h)	0-0
	6.12.05	Chelsea	(a)	0-0

First knockout round

	Date	Opponent		Score
1st leg	21.2.06	Benfica	(a)	0-1
2nd leg	8.3.06	Benfica	(h)	0-2

Aggregate score: 0-3

2006/07

Qualifying round

	Date	Opponent		Score
1st leg	8.8.06	Maccabi Haifa	(h)	2-1
2nd leg	22.8.06	Maccabi Haifa	(a)	1-1

Aggregate score: 3-2

Group phase

	Date	Opponent		Score
	12.9.06	PSV Eindhoven	(a)	0-0
	27.9.06	Galatasaray	(h)	3-2
	18.10.06	Bordeaux	(a)	1-0
	31.10.06	Bordeaux	(h)	3-0
	22.11.06	PSV Eindhoven	(h)	2-0
	5.12.06	Galatasaray	(a)	2-3

First knockout round

	Date	Opponent		Score
1st leg	21.2.07	Barcelona	(a)	2-1
2nd leg	6.3.07	Barcelona	(h)	0-1

Aggregate score: 2-2 (Liverpool win on away goals)

Quarter-final

	Date	Opponent		Score
1st leg	3.4.07	PSV Eindhoven	(a)	3-0
2nd leg	11.4.07	PSV Eindhoven	(h)	1-0

Aggregate score: 4-0

Semi-final

	Date	Opponent		Score
1st leg	25.4.07	Chelsea	(a)	0-1
2nd leg	1.5.07	Chelsea	(h)	1-0

Aggregate score: 1-1 (Liverpool win 4-1 on pens)

Final (Athens)

	Date	Opponent		Score
	23.5.07	AC Milan		1-2

2007/08

Qualifying round

	Date	Opponent		Score
1st leg	15.8.07	Toulouse	(a)	1-0
2nd leg	28.8.07	Toulouse	(h)	4-0

Aggregate score: 5-0

Group phase

	Date	Opponent		Score
	18.9.07	Porto	(a)	1-1
	3.10.07	Marseille	(h)	0-1
	24.10.07	Besiktas	(a)	1-2
	6.11.07	Besiktas	(h)	8-0
	28.11.07	Porto	(h)	4-1
	11.12.07	Marseille	(a)	4-0

First knockout round				
1st leg	19.2.08	Inter Milan	(h)	2-0
2nd leg	11.3.08	Inter Milan	(a)	1-0
Aggregate score: 3-0				
Quarter-final				
1st leg	2.4.08	Arsenal	(a)	1-1
2nd leg	8.4.08	Arsenal	(h)	4-2
Aggregate score: 5-3				
Semi-final				
1st leg	22.4.08	Chelsea	(h)	1-1
2nd leg	30.4.08	Chelsea	(a)	2-3
Aggregate score: 3-4				
2008/09				
Qualifying round				
1st leg	13.8.08	Standard Liege	(a)	0-0
2nd leg	27.8.08	Standard Liege	(h)	1-0
Aggregate score: 1-0				
Group phase				
	16.9.08	Marseille	(a)	2-1
	1.10.08	PSV Eindhoven	(h)	3-1
	22.10.08	Atletico Madrid	(a)	1-1
	4.11.08	Atletico Madrid	(h)	1-1
	26.11.08	Marseille	(h)	1-0
	9.12.08	PSV Eindhoven	(a)	3-1
First knockout round				
1st leg	25.2.09	Real Madrid	(a)	1-0
2nd leg	10.3.09	Real Madrid	(h)	4-0
Aggregate score: 5-0				
Quarter-final				
1st leg	8.4.09	Chelsea	(h)	1-3
2nd leg	14.4.09	Chelsea	(a)	4-4
Aggregate score: 5-7				
2009/10				
Group phase				
	16.9.09	Debrecen VSC	(h)	1-0
	29.9.09	Fiorentina	(a)	0-2
	20.10.09	Lyon	(h)	1-2
	4.11.09	Lyon	(a)	1-1
	24.11.09	Debrecen VSC	(a)	1-0
	9.12.09	Fiorentina	(h)	1-2
2014/15				
Group phase				
	16.9.14	Ludogorets Razgrad	(h)	2-1
	1.10.14	Basel	(a)	0-1
	22.10.14	Real Madrid	(h)	0-3
	4.11.14	Real Madrid	(a)	0-1
	26.11.14	Ludogorets Razgrad	(a)	2-2
	9.12.14	Basel	(h)	1-1

2017/18				
Qualifying round				
1st leg	15.8.17	TSG 1899 Hoffenheim	(a)	2-1
2nd leg	23.8.17	TSG 1899 Hoffenheim	(h)	4-2
Aggregate score: 6-3				
Group phase				
	13.9.17	Sevilla	(h)	2-2
	26.9.17	Spartak Moscow	(a)	1-1
	17.10.17	NK Maribor	(a)	7-0
	1.11.17	NK Maribor	(h)	3-0
	21.11.17	Sevilla	(a)	3-3
	6.12.17	Spartak Moscow	(h)	7-0
First knockout round				
1st leg	14.2.18	Porto	(a)	5-0
2nd leg	6.3.18	Porto	(h)	0-0
Aggregate score: 5-0				
Quarter-final				
1st leg	4.4.18	Manchester City	(h)	3-0
2nd leg	10.4.18	Manchester City	(a)	2-1
Aggregate score: 5-1				
Semi-final				
1st leg	24.4.18	AS Roma	(h)	5-2
2nd leg	2.5.18	AS Roma	(a)	2-4
Aggregate score: 7-6				
Final (Kiev)				
	26.5.18	Real Madrid		1-3
2018/19				
Group phase				
	18.9.18	Paris Saint-Germain	(h)	3-2
	3.10.18	Napoli	(a)	0-1
	24.10.18	Red Star Belgrade	(h)	4-0
	6.11.18	Red Star Belgrade	(a)	0-2
	28.11.18	Paris Saint-Germain	(a)	1-2
	11.12.18	Napoli	(h)	1-0
First knockout round				
1st leg	19.2.19	Bayern Munich	(h)	0-0
2nd leg	13.3.19	Bayern Munich	(a)	3-1
Aggregate score: 3-1				
Quarter-final				
1st leg	9.4.19	Porto	(h)	2-0
2nd leg	17.4.19	Porto	(a)	4-1
Aggregate score: 6-1				
Semi-final				
1st leg	1.5.19	Barcelona	(a)	0-3
2nd leg	7.5.19	Barcelona	(h)	4-0
Aggregate score: 4-3				
Final (Madrid)				
	1.6.19	Tottenham Hotspur		2-0

LIVERPOOL'S FAB FOUR

In leading Liverpool to Champions League glory in 2019, Jürgen Klopp joined an elite band of Anfield bosses. He is one of only four managers to have guided the Reds to the most coveted prize in club football. For this reason alone, his name will forever be etched in Liverpudlian folklore and he's not in bad company…

BOB PAISLEY

European Cups: 3 – 1977, 1978 & 1981
Born: Hetton-le-Hole, 23 January 1919
Liverpool manager: 1974 to 1983
Total number of games in charge: 535

Did you know? Paisley was the first manager to win the European Cup three times, a feat since emulated by Carlo Ancelotti and Zinedine Zidane.

"This is the second time I've beaten the Germans here… the first time was in 1944. I drove into Rome on a tank when the city was liberated. If anyone had told me I'd be back here to see us win the European Cup 33 years later I'd have told them they were mad! I want to savour every minute of it… which is why I'm not having a drink tonight. I'm just drinking in the occasion. Now we have achieved our greatest ambition." – **Paisley on the European Cup win of 1977.**

JOE FAGAN

European Cups: 1 - 1984
Born: Liverpool, 12 March 1921
Liverpool manager: 1983 to 1985
Total number of games in charge: 131

Did you know? Fagan, aged sixty-three years and seventy-nine days, was once the oldest manager to win the European Cup. It was an honour he held until 1993.

"My feelings about this are sincere. I am always sorry for any team beaten in a cup final, particularly a European Cup final. I feel for Roma and for their coach. But somebody has got to win – even on penalties. I am just delighted that we managed to do that tonight." **- Fagan on the European Cup win of 1984.**

RAFAEL BENITEZ

European Cups: 1 – 2005
Born: Madrid, 16 April 1960
Liverpool manager: 2004 to 2010
Total number of games in charge: 350

Did you know? Prior to becoming Liverpool manager, Benitez twice managed Valencia against the Reds in the Champions League – winning on both occasions.

"I was as delighted as anyone, though perhaps I was not as elaborate in my celebrations as some of the players. It is a mixture of relief - at having won when all seemed lost – and incredible pride at having achieved something you have worked so hard for, over the course of a season, over the course of a career." **- Benitez on the Champions League win of 2005.**

JÜRGEN KLOPP

European Cups: 1 – 2019
Born: Stuttgart, 16 June 1967
Liverpool manager: 2015 to present
Total number of games in charge: 208 (up to and including the 2019 CL final)

Did you know? Before leading Liverpool to victory in Madrid, Klopp had twice suffered the pain of defeat in a Champions League final – first with Borussia Dortmund in 2013 and then with Liverpool in 2018.

"Did you ever see a team like this, fighting with no fuel in the tank? I am so happy for the boys, all these people and my family. They suffer for me, they deserve it more than anybody. It was an intense season with the most beautiful finish I ever could have imagined." **- Klopp on the Champions League win of 2019.**

INTRODUCING THE 2018/19 CHAMPIONS OF EUROPE

A total of 20 players featured for Liverpool during the victorious 2018/19 Champions League campaign. Here are their vital statistics...

3 FABINHO

DOB: 23/10/93
Country: Brazil
Position: Midfield
Games: 11

Minutes: 727
Distance covered: 89009m
Passing accuracy: 68%
Crosses completed: 0

Clearances: 0
Tackles won: 21
Assists: 0
Goals: 0

4 VIRGIL VAN DIJK

DOB: 8/7/91
Country: Holland
Position: Defence
Games: 12

Minutes: 1080
Distance covered: 105914m
Passing accuracy: 89%
Crosses completed: 0

Clearances: 51
Tackles won: 4
Assists: 1
Goals: 2

5 GEORGINIO WIJNALDUM

DOB: 11/11/90
Country: Holland
Position: Midfield
Games: 12

Minutes: 971
Distance covered: 11754m
Passing accuracy: 87%
Crosses completed: 1

Clearances: 0
Tackles won: 0
Assists: 0
Goals: 2

6 DEJAN LOVREN

DOB: 5/7/89
Country: Croatia
Position: Defence
Games: 3

Minutes: 181
Distance covered: 19054m
Passing accuracy: 94%
Crosses completed: 0

Clearances: 5
Tackles won: 0
Assists: 0
Goals: 0

7 JAMES MILNER

DOB: 4/1/86   **Minutes:** 901   **Clearances:** 0
Country: England   **Distance covered:** 121642m   **Tackles won:** 6
Position: Midfield   **Passing accuracy:** 79%   **Assists:** 2
Games: 12   **Crosses completed:** 13   **Goals:** 2

8 NABY KEÏTA

DOB: 10/2/95   **Minutes:** 244   **Clearances:** 0
Country: Guinea   **Distance covered:** 29788m   **Tackles won:** 0
Position: Midfield   **Passing accuracy:** 75%   **Assists:** 0
Games: 6   **Crosses completed:** 0   **Goals:** 1

9 ROBERTO FIRMINO

DOB: 2/10/91   **Minutes:** 749   **Clearances:** 0
Country: Brazil   **Distance covered:** 95626m   **Tackles won:** 0
Position: Attack   **Passing accuracy:** 79%   **Assists:** 1
Games: 12   **Crosses completed:** 3   **Goals:** 4

10 SADIO MANÉ

DOB: 10/4/92   **Minutes:** 1152   **Clearances:** 0
Country: Senegal   **Distance covered:** 134826m   **Tackles won:** 1
Position: Attack   **Passing accuracy:** 72%   **Assists:** 1
Games: 13   **Crosses completed:** 3   **Goals:** 4

11 MOHAMED SALAH

DOB: 15/6/92   **Minutes:** 1058   **Clearances:** 0
Country: Egypt   **Distance covered:** 117578m   **Tackles won:** 0
Position: Attack   **Passing accuracy:** 67%   **Assists:** 2
Games: 12   **Crosses completed:** 5   **Goals:** 5

12 JOE GOMEZ

DOB: 23/5/97   **Minutes:** 525   **Clearances:** 15
Country: England   **Distance covered:** 58848m   **Tackles won:** 1
Position: Defence   **Passing accuracy:** 66%   **Assists:** 0
Games: 9   **Crosses completed:** 0   **Goals:** 0

13 ALISSON BECKER

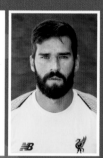

DOB: 2/10/92
Country: Brazil
Position: Goalkeeper

Games: 13
Minutes: 1170
Passing accuracy: 83%

Goals conceded: 12
Clean Sheets: 6
Saves: 46

14 JORDAN HENDERSON

DOB: 17/6/90
Country: England
Position: Midfield
Games: 11

Minutes: 799
Distance covered: 101797m
Passing accuracy: 84%
Crosses completed: 3

Clearances: 0
Tackles won: 3
Assists: 2
Goals: 0

15 DANIEL STURRIDGE

DOB: 1/9/89
Country: England
Position: Attack
Games: 7

Minutes: 163
Distance covered: 20831m
Passing accuracy: 75%
Crosses completed: 0

Clearances: 0
Tackles won: 0
Assists: 1
Goals: 1

18 ALBERTO MORENO

DOB: 5/7/92
Country: Spain
Position: Defence
Games: 1

Minutes: 8
Distance covered: 1282m
Passing accuracy: 100%
Crosses completed: 0

Clearances: 0
Tackles won: 0
Assists: 0
Goals: 0

20 ADAM LALLANA

DOB: 10/5/88
Country: England
Position: Midfield
Games: 3

Minutes: 104
Distance covered: 14229m
Passing accuracy: 88%
Crosses completed: 0

Clearances: 0
Tackles won: 0
Assists: 0
Goals: 0

23 XHERDAN SHAQIRI

DOB: 10/10/91
Country: Switzerland
Position: Midfield
Games: 4

Minutes: 176
Distance covered: 21761m
Passing accuracy: 63%
Crosses completed: 4

Clearances: 0
Tackles won: 1
Assists: 2
Goals: 0

26 ANDY ROBERTSON

DOB: 11/3/94
Country: Scotland
Position: Defender
Games: 12

Minutes: 1008
Distance covered: 113500m
Passing accuracy: 79%
Crosses completed: 6

Clearances: 27
Tackles won: 6
Assists: 2
Goals: 0

27 DIVOCK ORIGI

DOB: 18/4/95
Country: Belgium
Position: Attack
Games: 8

Minutes: 217
Distance covered: 28076m
Passing accuracy: 71%
Crosses completed: 2

Clearances: 0
Tackles won: 0
Assists: 0
Goals: 3

32 JOEL MATIP

DOB: 8/8/91
Country: Cameroon
Position: Defence
Games: 8

Minutes: 720
Distance covered: 75499m
Passing accuracy: 85%
Crosses completed: 0

Clearances: 21
Tackles won: 2
Assists: 1
Goals: 0

66 TRENT ALEXANDER-ARNOLD

DOB: 7/10/98
Country: England
Position: Defence
Games: 11

Minutes: 921
Distance covered: 103443m
Passing accuracy: 65%
Crosses completed: 23

Clearances: 24
Tackles won: 2
Assists: 4
Goals: 0

KIEV 2018

PAIN IN UKRAINE BUT LESSONS LEARNED

It's often been said that to fully enjoy the best of times you must first suffer the worst of times. In the case of Liverpool's most recent history in the Champions League, this certainly rings true. Before the glory of Madrid '19 came the pain of Kiev '18...

Twelve months prior to the Scouse Armada's invasion of Spain, the Red hordes descended on the capital of Ukraine in their thousands.

Optimism was high. Jürgen Klopp had taken the club back to Europe's top table for the first time in 11 years and this was hopefully going to be the crowning moment of a campaign that had seen progression beyond the wildest dreams of every Liverpudlian.

Sevilla, Spartak Moscow, NK Maribor, Porto, Manchester City and AS Roma had all been brushed aside during an unforgettable run to the final.

Standing in the way of Liverpool and a reunion with a long-lost friend though, was the mighty star-studded Real Madrid - winners of the competition for the previous two years and a team hellbent on making it three-in-a-row.

2018 CHAMPIONS LEAGUE FINAL

VENUE: NSC Olimpiyskiy Stadium, Kiev

DATE: Saturday 26 May 2018

ATTENDANCE: 61,561

REFEREE: Milorad Mazic (Serbia)

RESULT:

Liverpool 1
Real Madrid 3

GOALS

0-1 Benzema '51
1-1 Mané '55
1-2 Bale '64
1-3 Bale '83

TEAMS:

LIVERPOOL: Loris Karius, Virgil Van Dijk, Dejan Lovren, Andrew Robertson, Trent Alexander-Arnold, Georginio Wijnaldum, James Milner (Emre Can '83), Jordan Henderson, Sadio Mané, Mohamed Salah (Adam Lallana '31), Roberto Firmino.

REAL MADRID: Keylor Navas, Dani Carvajal (Nacho '37), Sergio Ramos, Raphael Varane, Marcelo, Luka Modric, Carlos Henrique Casimiro, Toni Kroos, Isco (Gareth Bale '61), Karim Benzema (Marco Asensio '89), Cristiano Ronaldo.

So near. Yet so far. Tears were unashamedly shed. However, heads remained high.

What happened that night in Kiev's Olympic Stadium would stand the 2019 winners in good stead, but at the time it was a bitter pill to swallow.

Despite Sadio Mané joining that illustrious band of Liverpool players to have scored in a European Cup final, two goalkeeping errors and one of the most spectacular goals that has ever been scored on this grand stage consigned the Reds to defeat.

And while their conquerors cavorted with the prize that they had so dearly coveted, a steely determination to right those wrongs was being instilled.

Little did Jürgen Klopp, his players or the supporters know that the chance to make amends would come around again so soon.

It may not have seemed so at the time, but this was a valuable learning curve and where the story of number six began.

UEFA CHAMPIONS LEAGUE

2018/19 GROUP PHASE DRAW

The draw for the group phase of the 2018/19 Champions League took place in Monaco on 30 August 2018. 32 teams were drawn into eight groups of four, with Liverpool placed in Group C, as the third ranked team.

The top seeded side in the group was PSG, the dominant force in French football and one of the pre-tournament favourites. Next to be drawn out was Italian giants Napoli, runners-up in Serie A the previous season. And completing the line-up was Red Star Belgrade of Serbia, European Cup winners in 1991 but competing in the group phase of the Champions League for the first time after battling their way through four qualifying rounds.

Jürgen Klopp's reaction to the draw: "I expected a difficult group, we have a difficult group and that's what the Champions League is all about. The Champions League is the biggest club competition in the world, so it should be difficult because it is. PSG are one of the most exciting teams in the world and I think their target is to win the Champions League, so that will be two interesting matches. Napoli, we beat them in pre-season but it goes without saying these two games will be completely a different challenge. I've been to Napoli with Dortmund, so I know what the atmosphere is like there. Red Star, I watched them last night. They came through and it will be, again, a very, very intense atmosphere I am sure."

GROUP A
ATLETICO MADRID
(SPAIN)
BORUSSIA DORTMUND
(GERMANY)
MONACO
(FRANCE)
CLUB BRUGGE
(BELGIUM)

GROUP B
BARCELONA
(SPAIN)
TOTTENHAM
(ENGLAND)
PSV EINDHOVEN
(HOLLAND)
INTERNAZIONALE
(ITALY)

GROUP C
PARIS ST GERMAIN
(FRANCE)
NAPOLI
(ITALY)
LIVERPOOL
(ENGLAND)
RED STAR BELGRADE
(SERBIA)

GROUP D
LOKOMOTIV MOSCOW
(RUSSIA)
PORTO
(PORTUGAL)
SCHALKE
(GERMANY)
GALATASARAY
(TURKEY)

GROUP E
BAYERN MUNICH
(GERMANY)
BENFICA
(PORTUGAL)
AJAX
(HOLLAND)
AEK ATHENS
(GREECE)

GROUP F
MANCHESTER CITY
(ENGLAND)
SHAKHTAR DONETSK
(UKRAINE)
LYON
(FRANCE)
HOFFENHEIM
(GERMANY)

GROUP G
REAL MADRID
(SPAIN)
AS ROMA
(ITALY)
CSKA MOSCOW
(RUSSIA)
VIKTORIA PLZEN
(CZECH REPUBLIC)

GROUP H
JUVENTUS
(ITALY)
MANCHESTER UNITED
(ENGLAND)
VALENCIA
(SPAIN)
YOUNG BOYS
(SWITZERLAND)

MATCHDAY ONE
LIVERPOOL V PARIS SAINT-GERMAIN

VENUE: Anfield

DATE: Tuesday 18 September 2018

ATTENDANCE: 52,478

REFEREE: Cuneyt Cakir (Turkey)

RESULT:

Liverpool 3
Paris Saint-Germain 2

GOALS

1-0 Sturridge '30
2-0 Milner '36 (penalty)
1-2 Meunier '40
2-2 Mbappe '83
3-2 Firmino '90

LIVERPOOL: Alisson Becker, Virgil Van Dijk, Joe Gomez, Andrew Robertson, Trent Alexander-Arnold, Georginio Wijnaldum, James Milner, Jordan Henderson, Sadio Mané (Fabinho Tavarez '90), Mohamed Salah (Xherdan Shaqiri '85), Daniel Sturridge (Roberto Firmino '72).

PSG: Alphonse Areola, Thomas Meunier, Thiago Silva, Presnel Kimpembe, Juan Bernat, Adrien Rabiot, Marquinhos, Angel Di Maria (Eric Maxim Choupo-Moting '80), Kylian Mbappe, Edinson Cavani (Julian Draxler '80), Neymar da Silva Santos Junior.

MATCH OVERVIEW

Liverpool got their Champions League campaign off to a winning start in the most dramatic of circumstances. A flying start from the Reds saw them race into a two-goal lead courtesy of Daniel Sturridge's header and a James Milner penalty; however, Thomas Meunier pulled one back for the French champions before half-time. The hosts dominated the second period, but PSG levelled with their first shot on goal after the break as Kylian Mbappe swept in. But, having come off the bench, Roberto Firmino won it in stoppage-time when he drilled home the winner.

POST-MATCH REACTION

Jürgen Klopp: "It was good, really good in all departments pretty much. It is so difficult to defend them, but we did. Good organisation and a big heart is always a good combination for defending. All 11 players were involved in that. A good performance against an outstandingly strong opponent; it was necessary we played good. The atmosphere was fantastic, so special to do these things in this stadium. It was nice."

MATCH STATS

LIVERPOOL		PSG
3	GOALS	2
17	ATTEMPTS	9
51%	POSSESSION	49%
13	CORNERS	1
1	OFFSIDES	2
82%	PASSING ACCURACY	89%
104.2KM	DISTANCE COVERED	101.3KM

GROUP C TABLE

	CLUB	P	W	D	L	GF	GA	Pts
1	LIVERPOOL FC	1	1	0	0	3	2	3
2	RED STAR BELGRADE	1	0	1	0	0	0	1
3	NAPOLI	1	0	1	0	0	0	1
4	PARIS SAINT-GERMAIN	1	0	0	1	2	3	0

MATCHDAY TWO
NAPOLI V LIVERPOOL

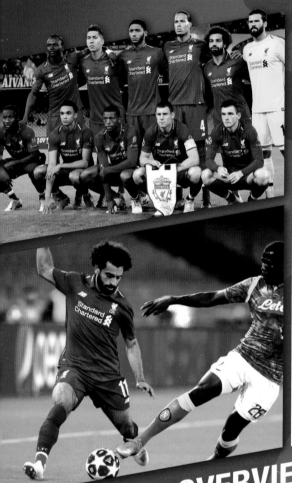

VENUE: Stadio San Paolo, Naples

DATE: Wednesday 3 October 2018

ATTENDANCE: 37,057

REFEREE: Viktor Kassai (Hungary)

RESULT: Napoli 1 Liverpool 0

GOALS 1-0 Insigne '90

NAPOLI: David Ospina, Nikola Maksimovic, Raul Albiol, Kalidou Koulibaly, Mario Rui, Jose Callejon, Allan, Marek Hamsik (Piotr Zielinski '81), Fabian Ruiz Pena (Simone Verdi '68), Lorenzo Insigne, Arkadiusz Milik (Dries Mertens '68).

LIVERPOOL: Alisson Becker, Virgil Van Dijk, Joe Gomez, Andrew Robertson, Trent Alexander-Arnold, Georginio Wijnaldum, James Milner (Fabinho Tavarez '76), Naby Keïta (Jordan Henderson '18), Roberto Firmino, Sadio Mané (Daniel Sturridge '88), Mohamed Salah.

MATCH OVERVIEW

On a frustrating night in Naples, Liverpool were felled by a last-gasp goal just when it looked like a resolute defensive performance would be enough to earn them a point. The Reds were, admittedly, not at their best and suffered an early blow when Keïta went off injured. A below-par display was summed up in the fact that they failed to register a single shot on target and they eventually paid the price. Napoli upped the pressure in the second half, with Gomez having to clear off the line and Mertens rattling the crossbar before Insigne turned home a 90th minute Callejon cross to claim the victory for the Italians.

POST-MATCH REACTION

Jürgen Klopp: "There was not that much pressure from Napoli, it feels like if you looked at how we played then it looked like they were constantly on us, but it was not like this. We could've played really calmer, prepared the situations better but we didn't, so we didn't create a lot of chances. First half was kind of OK, but second half was not good enough. It's always a bad sign if you have to say your goalkeeper was your best player, but that was obvious tonight. Then in the last minute, we made another tactical mistake and that's the problem."

MATCH STATS

NAPOLI		LIVERPOOL
1	GOALS	0
16	ATTEMPTS	4
55%	POSSESSION	45%
5	CORNERS	1
7	OFFSIDES	1
89%	PASSING ACCURACY	81%
112.1KM	DISTANCE COVERED	112.9KM

GROUP C TABLE

	CLUB	P	W	D	L	GF	GA	Pts
1	NAPOLI	2	1	1	0	1	0	4
2	LIVERPOOL	2	1	0	1	3	3	3
3	PARIS SAINT-GERMAIN	2	1	0	1	8	4	3
4	RED STAR BELGRADE	2	0	1	1	1	6	1

THERE ARE PLACES I REMEMBER...
ROME 1977

PAISLEY'S REDS MUNCH ON GLADBACH

On a truly historic night in Rome, Liverpool got their hands on the European Cup for the first time.

It was the culmination of 13 years' endeavour and an occasion that will forever be regarded as one of the greatest in the club's history.

Coming just four days after Bob Paisley and his players had seen their treble dreams dashed in the FA Cup final, it was also the ultimate high on which to end an incredible season.

Backed by the amazing support of over 26,000 travelling Liverpudlians whose sea of red and white chequered flags formed a kaleidoscope of colour

VENUE: Stadio Olimpico, Rome

DATE: 25 May 1977

ATTENDANCE: 56,000

RESULT: Liverpool 3 Borussia M'gladbach 1

GOALS
McDermott (1-0 '27), Simonsen (1-1 '51), Smith (2-1 '64), Neal (3-1 pen '82)

LIVERPOOL: Clemence, Neal, Jones, Smith, Kennedy, Hughes, Keegan, Case, Heighway, McDermott, Callaghan.

BORUSSIA MOENCHENGLADBACH: Kneib, Vogts, Wittkamp, Schaffer, Klinkhammer, Bonhof, Wohlers, Stielike, Wimmer (Kulik '24), Simonsen, Heynckes.

at the Stadio Olimpico, Liverpool took to the field in a confident mood and went ahead through Terry McDermott's sweetly struck 27th minute goal.

A rare lapse in concentration allowed Allan Simonsen to draw the Germans level shortly after the break, and only a fine stop by Ray Clemence denied them a second as the pendulum threatened to swing in their favour.

Stung back into action by Borussia's brief spell of dominance Liverpool regained the upper hand midway through the second-half. Tommy Smith, on what was supposedly his last game before retirement, rose majestically to meet a Steve Heighway corner and powered home a header that gave the 'keeper no chance.

Eight minutes from time Phil Neal added the finishing touch to the most momentous of victories, calmly side-footing home from the penalty spot after Bertie Vogts had fouled Kevin Keegan.

At last, Liverpool Football Club could proudly call themselves the undisputed Kings of Europe.

MATCHDAY THREE
LIVERPOOL V RED STAR BELGRADE

VENUE: Anfield

DATE: Wednesday 24 October 2018

ATTENDANCE: 53,024

REFEREE: Daniel Siebert (Germany)

RESULT:
Liverpool 4
Red Star Belgrade 0

GOALS
1-0 Firmino '20
2-0 Salah '45
3-0 Salah '51 (penalty)
4-0 Mané '79

LIVERPOOL: Alisson Becker, Virgil Van Dijk, Joe Gomez, Andrew Robertson (Alberto Moreno '82), Trent Alexander-Arnold, Fabinho Tavarez, Georginio Wijnaldum, Xherdan Shaqiri (Adam Lallana '68), Roberto Firmino, Sadio Mané, Mohamed Salah (Daniel Sturridge '73).

RED STAR: Milan Borjan, Filip Stojkovic, Milos Degenek, Srdan Babic, Marko Gobeljic, Nenad Krsticic, Branko Jovicic (Goran Causic '75), Ben Nabouhane (Veljko Simic '81), Lorenzo Ebecilio (Dusan Jovancic '65), Slavoljub Srnic, Richmond Boakye.

MATCH OVERVIEW

Liverpool got back to winning ways in emphatic fashion and moved to the top of Group C in the process. In what was the first meeting between these two sides since 1973 – when Red Star dumped Bill Shankly's Liverpool out of the European Cup – it was the home side who held the upper hand from start to finish. Liverpool went ahead thanks to a deflected shot from Firmino after 20 minutes and from then on the result was never in doubt. A Salah double either side of the interval extended the lead and Mané missed a penalty before completing the rout 11 minutes from time.

POST-MATCH REACTION

Jürgen Klopp: "I think Red Star did a really good job, but we were really good tonight and that makes it difficult. We did the right things in the right moments and that's how you can win games. It was just a good game, a good football game and they could finish the situations because we had the right movements in the right moment. In the first two goals we had the counter-pressing situations, which is brilliant and very important. When you see how big the impact of the boys coming on, that's really important as well. You can't win 4-0 if most of the things are not good, and tonight most of the things were really good."

MATCH STATS

LIVERPOOL		RED STAR
4	GOALS	0
22	ATTEMPTS	3
61%	POSSESSION	39%
4	CORNERS	1
4	OFFSIDES	2
89%	PASSING ACCURACY	71%
108.4KM	DISTANCE COVERED	111.5KM

GROUP C TABLE

	CLUB	P	W	D	L	GF	GA	Pts
1	LIVERPOOL	3	2	0	1	7	3	6
2	NAPOLI	3	1	2	0	3	2	5
3	PARIS SAINT-GERMAIN	3	1	1	1	10	6	4
4	RED STAR BELGRADE	3	0	1	2	1	10	1

MATCHDAY FOUR
RED STAR BELGRADE V LIVERPOOL

RED STAR: Milan Borjan, Filip Stojkovic (Marko Gobeljic '59), Vujadan Savic, Milos Degenek, Milan Rodic, Nenad Krsticic (Branko Jovicic '73), Dusan Jovancic, Ben Nabouhane, Marko Marin (Goran Causic '64), Slavoljub Srnic, Milan Pavkov.

LIVERPOOL: Alisson Becker, Virgil Van Dijk, Andrew Robertson, Joel Matip, Trent Alexander-Arnold (Joe Gomez '46), Georginio Wijnaldum, James Milner, Adam Lallana (Divock Origi '79), Sadio Mané, Mohamed Salah, Daniel Sturridge (Roberto Firmino '46).

VENUE: Stadion Rajko Mitic, Belgrade

DATE: Tuesday 6 November 2018

ATTENDANCE: 51,318

REFEREE: Antonio Mateu Lahoz (Spain)

RESULT: Red Star Belgrade 2 Liverpool 0

GOALS
1-0 Pavkov '22
2-0 Pavkov '29

MATCH OVERVIEW

Liverpool crashed to a shock second away defeat of the campaign and, come the final whistle, could have no complaints about the eventual outcome. After Sturridge spurned a good chance when the score was still goalless, the home side struck twice in quick succession through Pavkov; the first a bullet header, the second a spectacular long-range effort. It was enough to secure the first-ever win for a Serbian side in the Champions League group stage and it meant Liverpool's lead at the top of the table had been cut to just goal difference. With two games to go, the race for qualification was now wide open.

POST-MATCH REACTION

Jürgen Klopp: "We were not surprised by Red Star's tactics. In Liverpool we controlled the game, tonight we didn't. We made life a bit too easy tonight, that's the problem. They deserved it for the passion they showed. We have to admit - congratulations Red Star, it was well deserved. They have the three points, we have nothing. The start was intense, that was clear. Red Star wanted to strike back, which they did. We had the first big chance with Daniel, a very big one. Each goal in a game like this leads the game in a specific direction. We tried to change for the second half. We had moments, we had kind of nearly-chances, the biggest in the last two, three minutes and before that not enough."

MATCH STATS

RED STAR		LIVERPOOL
	GOALS	0
2	ATTEMPTS	22
10	POSSESSION	65%
35%	CORNERS	9
5	OFFSIDES	4
0	PASSING ACCURACY	85%
66%	DISTANCE COVERED	109.8KM
115.6KM		

GROUP C TABLE

	CLUB	P	W	D	L	GF	GA	Pts
1	LIVERPOOL	4	2	0	2	7	5	6
2	NAPOLI	4	2	0	2	4	3	6
3	PARIS SAINT-GERMAIN	4	1	3	0	11	7	5
4	RED STAR BELGRADE	4	1	2	1	3	10	4

THERE ARE PLACES I REMEMBER...
WEMBLEY 1978

KING KENNY KOPS THE CUP

Just twelve months after lifting the European Cup for the first time Liverpool became the first British side to retain the trophy on a memorable night at Wembley.

As reigning champions, and with the added advantage of playing in their home country, they were overwhelming favourites to lift the cup again. Kevin Keegan had gone but in Kenny Dalglish Reds fans had found themselves a new hero to worship. Dalglish had enjoyed a great first season with the club and this was to be his crowning moment.

As a contest it may not have been as memorable as the previous season's victory in Rome but for those involved it was still an occasion to savour.

Straight from the first whistle it was evident that Club Brugge were content to defend, making for a one-sided but frustrating encounter.

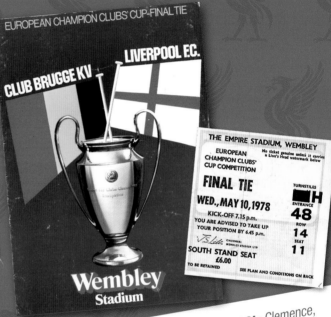

VENUE: Wembley Stadium, London

DATE: 10 May 1978

ATTENDANCE: 92,500

RESULT: Liverpool 1 Club Brugge 0

GOALS Dalglish (1-0 '65)

LIVERPOOL: Clemence, Neal, Thompson, Hansen, Kennedy, Hughes, Dalglish, Case, Fairclough, McDermott, Souness.

CLUB BRUGGE: Jensen, Bastijns, Krieger, Leekens, Maes (Volders '71), Cools, de Cubber, Ku (Sanders '60), Vandereycken, Sorenson, Simoen.

Thankfully, such negativity eventually got what it deserved and when the breakthrough finally came, no-one could begrudge Liverpool their strike.

What turned out to be the only goal of the game arrived in the 65th minute, with new boys Souness and Dalglish combining to break the deadlock, the latter finishing the move with a superbly executed chip over the 'keeper.

Given their total supremacy it was a goal in-keeping with the run of play and apart from a late scare when Phil Thompson was forced to clear off the line the Reds never looked in danger of surrendering their lead.

The final whistle sparked delirious scenes of joy beneath the twin towers. The club had created history and the jubilant Liverpool fans vociferously acclaimed their double European Cup winning heroes.

MATCHDAY FIVE
PARIS SAINT-GERMAIN V LIVERPOOL

VENUE: Parc des Princes, Paris

DATE: Wednesday 28 November 2018

ATTENDANCE: 46,880

REFEREE: Szymon Marciniak (Poland)

RESULT:
Paris Saint-Germain 2
Liverpool 1

GOALS
1-0 Bernat '13
2-0 Neymar '37
2-1 Milner '45

PSG: Gianluigi Buffon, Thilo Kehrer, Thiago Silva, Presnel Kimpembe, Juan Bernat, Angel Di Maria (Dani Alves '65), Marquinhos, Marco Verratti, Neymar da Silva Santos Junior, Kylian Mbappe (Adrien Rabiot '85), Edinson Cavani (Eric Maxim Choupo-Moting '65).

LIVERPOOL: Alisson Becker, Virgil Van Dijk, Dejan Lovren, Joe Gomez, Andrew Robertson, Georginio Wijnaldum (Naby Keïta '66), James Milner (Xherdan Shaqiri '77), Jordan Henderson, Roberto Firmino (Daniel Sturridge '71), Sadio Mané, Mohamed Salah.

MATCH OVERVIEW

Liverpool's hopes of progressing to the round of 16 were left hanging in the balance after this disappointing defeat in the French capital. The hosts scored twice before Milner reduced the deficit with a penalty on the stroke of half-time. However, it wasn't enough to spark a comeback and despite dominating for long periods of the second-half, the Reds failed to muster an equaliser and therefore slipped to third in the table, meaning the race for qualification would not be decided until the final matchday.

POST-MATCH REACTION

Jürgen Klopp: "It was a very important game for us and it was clear the start would be like the start was, especially when you saw their line-up. The approach they chose was full-risk, especially in the beginning – try everything as long as your legs carry you. With the quality they have it was quite intense to deal with."

MATCH STATS

PSG		LIVERPOOL
		1
	GOALS	7
2	ATTEMPTS	53%
12	POSSESSION	5
47%	CORNERS	1
5	OFFSIDES	85%
6	PASSING ACCURACY	106.4KM
85%	DISTANCE COVERED	
105.0KM		

GROUP C TABLE

	CLUB	P	W	D	L	GF	GA	Pts
1	NAPOLI	5	2	3	0	7	4	9
2	PARIS SAINT-GERMAIN	5	2	2	1	13	8	8
3	LIVERPOOL FC	5	2	0	3	8	7	6
4	RED STAR BELGRADE	5	1	1	3	4	13	4

MATCHDAY SIX
LIVERPOOL V NAPOLI

VENUE: Anfield

DATE: Tuesday 11 December 2018

ATTENDANCE: 52,015

REFEREE: Damir Skomina (Slovenia)

RESULT:
Liverpool 1
Napoli 0

GOALS
1-0 Salah '34

LIVERPOOL: Alisson Becker, Virgil Van Dijk, Andrew Robertson, Joel Matip, Trent Alexander-Arnold (Dejan Lovren '90), Georginio Wijnaldum, James Milner (Fabinho Tavarez '85), Jordan Henderson, Roberto Firmino (Naby Keïta '79), Sadio Mané, Mohamed Salah.

NAPOLI: David Ospina, Nikola Maksimovic, Raul Albiol, Kalidou Koulibaly, Mario Rui (Faouzi Ghoulam '70), Jose Callejon, Allan, Marek Hamsik, Fabian Ruiz Pena (Piotr Zielinski '62), Lorenzo Insigne, Dries Mertens (Arkadiusz Milik '67).

MATCH OVERVIEW

Liverpool secured their place in the last 16 of the Champions League on a memorable night at Anfield, doing what was necessary to leapfrog Napoli in the Group C table and claim second place. Needing either a 1-0 win or victory by a cushion of two goals or more, the stakes were high and a tense 90 minutes ensued. The vital breakthrough came just after the half-hour mark when Salah beat Ospina at the near post but the game – and progress to the next round – remained very much in the balance until the final whistle blew. The visitors would have snatched the point they required had it not been for a miraculous save by Alisson that denied Milik from point-blank range in the second minute of injury time.

POST-MATCH REACTION

Jürgen Klopp: "This game was just amazing, it was outstanding… unbelievable. The boys played with their whole heart on the pitch; with each part of their body they were in that game. Our offensive defending, our offensive pressing was some of the best I ever saw. The most difficult period was directly after the 1-0. You could see this little bit of relief and then immediately Napoli were there. That made the game so intense. After 65 minutes it was really wild from both sides – counter, counter, counter, counter – and quick transitions without really finishing. The goal Mo scored… what a goal! Unbelievable. And the save Ali made, I have no words for that. That was a life-saver tonight. I'm really proud of what the boys did tonight."

MATCH STATS

LIVERPOOL		NAPOLI
	GOALS	0
1	ATTEMPTS	8
23	POSSESSION	50%
50%	CORNERS	3
3	OFFSIDES	4
5	PASSING ACCURACY	77%
80%	DISTANCE COVERED	114.7KM
118.8KM		

GROUP C TABLE

	CLUB	P	W	D	L	GF	GA	Pts
1	PARIS SAINT-GERMAIN	6	3	2	1	17	9	11
2	LIVERPOOL	6	3	0	3	9	7	9
3	NAPOLI	6	2	3	1	7	5	9
4	RED STAR BELGRADE	6	1	1	4	5	17	4

THERE ARE PLACES I REMEMBER...
PARIS 1981

BARNEY RUBBLE SEALS NUMBER THREE IN GAY PAREE

The Reds joined an elite band of clubs to have won the European Cup three times with a hard-earned victory against the team that had dominated the competition in its formative years.

Liverpool versus Real Madrid was viewed as the classic final, the original Kings of Europe against the new pretenders to their throne.

It was a spectacle, however, that ultimately didn't live up to expectations and a first-half of few opportunities gave a packed Parc des Princes stadium little to get excited about.

Real included flamboyant English winger Laurie Cunningham in their starting eleven but in a bruising contest dominated by tight marking and tough tackling he failed to shine.

Liverpool's main danger-men were also unable to make their mark and some unruly Spanish cynicism resulted in at least a couple leaving the field with ripped shirts and socks.

VENUE: Parc des Princes, Paris

DATE: 27 May 1981

ATTENDANCE: 48,360

RESULT: Liverpool 1 Real Madrid 0

GOALS A Kennedy (1-0 '81)

LIVERPOOL: Clemence, Neal, A Kennedy, Thompson, Hansen, R Kennedy, Lee, McDermott, Souness, Dalglish (Case '86), Johnson.

REAL MADRID: Agustin, Cortes (Pineda '85), Camacho, Stielike, Sabido, del Bosque, Angel, Santillana, Navajas, Juanito, Cunningham.

The longer the game went without a goal the more both teams became engulfed by the fear factor and extra-time looked certain until an unlikely source popped up to score the winning goal with just nine minutes remaining.

From a throw-in on the left Ray Kennedy picked out his namesake Alan and the full-back barged through the Madrid defence before unleashing an angled shot that beat the 'keeper at his near post.

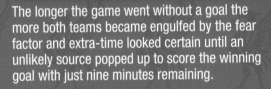

Cue a galloping foray over the advertising hoardings to celebrate with the ecstatic flag-waving Scouse hordes behind the goal.

Phil Thompson had the honour of lifting the club's third European Cup and Paris was later painted red as manager Bob Paisley took his place among the footballing immortals.

ROUND OF 16 1ST LEG
LIVERPOOL V BAYERN MUNICH

VENUE: Anfield

DATE: Tuesday 19 February 2019

ATTENDANCE: 52,250

REFEREE: Gianluca Rocchi (Italy)

RESULT: Liverpool 0 Bayern Munich 0

LIVERPOOL: Alisson Becker, Andrew Robertson, Joel Matip, Trent Alexander-Arnold, Fabinho Tavarez, Georginio Wijnaldum, Naby Keïta (James Milner '76), Jordan Henderson, Roberto Firmino (Divock Origi '76), Sadio Mané, Mohamed Salah.

BAYERN MUNICH: Manuel Neuer, Joshua Kimmich, Niklas Sule, Mats Hummels, David Alaba, Javi Martinez, Thiago Alcantara, Serge Gnabry (Rafinha '90), James Rodriguez (Renato Sanches '88), Kingsley Coman (Franck Ribery '81), Robert Lewandowski.

MATCH OVERVIEW

Considering the pre-match hype that had surrounded this eagerly anticipated clash between these two five-time European Cup winners, it was ultimately a game that failed to live up to expectations. On a cold and wet night, both sides cancelled each other out in a tough and physical encounter. Liverpool had the better chances but a resolute defensive display by the visitors reduced the Reds to just two shots on target. Although there was a sense of anti-climax about the occasion, tactically it was an intriguing tussle. In the end a draw was a fair result and it meant the tie remained evenly poised at the half-way point.

POST-MATCH REACTION

Jürgen Klopp: "It's not the result or the game we dreamed of. Not really a lot of things happened in the game but it was an intense one. There was a lot of respect involved in the game and that made life uncomfortable. Our problem tonight was, on one hand the quality of the opponent of course, but on the other hand our last pass was not our friend. We had 10 or 12 situations where everything was prepared, everything was on a plate, and then we played a very average last pass or gave it away. That caused us two problems; one, we didn't create a chance, and on the other hand we gave them the ball and they had a counter-attack, which made the game even more intense. I'm pretty sure at the moment Bayern feel a bit better than we do but it's 0-0, the best draw you can get. It will be a tough one again to play at Bayern. So it's not perfect but good enough to work with."

Jordan Henderson: "It's still alive. We've got games before the second leg. We've got to be confident still. It'll be difficult but we have experience in the Champions League."

Niko Kovac (Bayern Munich coach): "I can't remember that many clubs that have not lost and not conceded at Anfield. Liverpool, they are a sensationally good team. We're at home now and home games are an advantage."

MATCH STATS

LIVERPOOL		BAYERN MUNICH
	GOALS	0
0	ATTEMPTS	9
16	POSSESSION	53%
47%	CORNERS	6
5	OFFSIDES	2
1	PASSING ACCURACY	85%
80%	DISTANCE COVERED	111.8KM
118.8KM		

ROUND OF 16 2ND LEG

BAYERN MUNICH V LIVERPOOL

VENUE: Allianz Arena, Munich

DATE: Wednesday 13 March 2019

ATTENDANCE: 68,145

REFEREE: Daniele Orsato (Italy)

RESULT:
Bayern Munich 1
Liverpool 3

GOALS
0-1 Mané '26
1-1 Matip '39 (own goal)
1-2 Van Dijk '69
1-3 Mané '84

BAYERN MUNICH: Manuel Neuer, Rafinha, Niklas Sule, Mats Hummels, David Alaba, Javi Martinez (Leon Goretzka '72), Thiago Alcantara, James Rodriguez (Renato Sanches '79), Serge Gnabry, Franck Ribery (Kingsley Coman '61), Robert Lewandowski.

LIVERPOOL: Alisson Becker, Virgil Van Dijk, Andrew Robertson, Joel Matip, Trent Alexander-Arnold, Georginio Wijnaldum, James Milner (Adam Lallana '87), Jordan Henderson (Fabinho Tavarez '13), Roberto Firmino (Divock Origi '83), Sadio Mané, Mohamed Salah.

MATCH OVERVIEW

An outstanding European away performance saw Liverpool convincingly book their place in the Champions League quarter-final. A stunning finish from Mané, following a sublime through ball by Van Dijk, put them ahead in the tie and, although a Matip own goal meant the German champions were soon back on level terms, it was the visitors who always looked the more threatening. A towering Van Dijk header restored Liverpool's advantage midway through the second-half before Mané nodded in his second of the night to seal a famous victory.

POST-MATCH REACTION

Jürgen Klopp: "It's massive, a big step for us - a big, big, big one for us. We will see what we can do with it, but it is still fantastic sign that we again set a mark for LFC, for this wonderful club, that we really are back on the landscape of international, top-class football. We all think that's where this club belongs and tonight we proved it a little bit. In the moment, you can hear it, I am really happy about the result and the fact we are through. It is a difficult place to come and not a lot of teams have on their cards an away win at Munich. We have that now and that's cool. Difficult but cool. It is not that I expected it - I knew we had a chance, but I didn't expect it would happen, that it really would work out. The boys made it happen and that's brilliant, absolutely brilliant."

James Milner: "Great performance. Great result. Great night. Thanks to the travelling fans in the heavens."

Mats Hummels: "I know Jürgen Klopp and he is very good at eliminating the opponents' strengths and he showed that again today. The 1-2 took away our belief. After that Liverpool was the better team."

MATCH STATS

BAYERN		LIVERPOOL
	GOALS	3
1	ATTEMPTS	9
6	POSSESSION	41%
59%	CORNERS	7
2	OFFSIDES	2
5	PASSING ACCURACY	79%
86%	DISTANCE COVERED	115.4KM
113.0KM		

THERE ARE PLACES I REMEMBER...

NUMBER FOUR

ROME 1984

FAGAN'S TREBLE CHASERS MAKE ROMAN RUINS

The odds were stacked against Liverpool like never before ahead of the 1984 European Cup Final. Not only were the Reds taking on the reigning champions of Italy's Serie A, they had to do so on AS Roma's own ground.

In the best Anfield traditions though, the club simply got on with the task in hand and memorably conquered Rome for a second time.

The ultra-confident visitors drew first blood through Phil Neal, the only survivor from the first European Cup Final seven years previous, only for Roberto Pruzzo to level for the hosts shortly before the interval.

VENUE: Stadio Olimpico, Rome

DATE: 30 May 1984

ATTENDANCE: 69,693

RESULT: Liverpool 1 AS Roma 1 (Liverpool win 4-2 on penalties)

GOALS Neal (1-0 '14), Pruzzo (1-1 '44)

LIVERPOOL: Grobbelaar, Neal, Kennedy, Lawrenson, Hansen, Whelan, Lee, Johnston (Nicol '73), Souness, Dalglish (Robinson '95), Rush.

AS ROMA: Tancredi, Nappi, Righetti, Bonetti, Nela, Cerezo (Strukelj '115), Falcao, Di Bartolomei, Conti, Pruzzo (Chierico '63), Graziani.

After that there was little to separate the two teams and for the first time ever the European Cup final was to be decided by a penalty shoot-out.

It was to be the most nail-biting climax to a season yet and when Steve Nicol blazed over with the first kick, Liverpudlian hearts sunk.

Roma skipper Di Bartolemei made no mistake with his effort and the vociferous home support was in a jubilant mood.

Neal levelled the scores and then Conti missed to put Liverpool back in the match. Souness and Righetti also both converted before Ian Rush converted.

Bruce Grobbelaar's now famous 'wobbly legs' put Graziani off and the pendulum suddenly swung in Liverpool's favour.

The mathematics were simple – if Alan Kennedy scored, Liverpool would be European Champions for a fourth time.

Amid unbearable tension up he stepped and with his left foot he sent Tancredi the wrong way to spark delirious scenes of joy among the Liverpool players and supporters.

QUARTER-FINAL 1ST LEG
LIVERPOOL V PORTO

VENUE: Anfield

DATE: Tuesday 9 April 2019

ATTENDANCE: 52,465

REFEREE: Antonio Mateu Lahoz (Spain)

RESULT:
Liverpool 2
Porto 0

GOALS
1-0 Keïta '5
2-0 Firmino '26

LIVERPOOL: Alisson Becker, Virgil Van Dijk, Dejan Lovren, Trent Alexander-Arnold, Fabinho Tavarez, James Milner, Naby Keïta, Jordan Henderson, Roberto Firmino (Daniel Sturridge '82), Sadio Mané (Divock Origi '73), Mohamed Salah.

PORTO: Iker Casillas, Maxi Pereira (Fernando Andrade dos Santos '77), Felipe, Eder Militao, Jesus Manuel Corona, Danilo Pereira, Oliver Torres (Bruno Costa '73), Alex Telles, Otavio, Tiquinho Soares (Yacine Brahimi '62), Moussa Marega.

MATCH OVERVIEW

Porto came to Anfield looking to avenge their heavy defeat to the Reds in the previous season's competition, but their hopes were all but extinguished inside the opening half hour. The game was just five minutes old when Keïta netted his first European goal for the club to give Liverpool the perfect start. After Firmino doubled the advantage the result never looked in any real doubt although Porto refused to throw the towel in and went close on a number of occasions, denied only by the brilliance of Alisson. Mané had a goal disallowed for offside early in the second-half and Liverpool were unable to add to their tally but had given themselves a comfortable cushion ahead of the return leg.

POST-MATCH REACTION

Jürgen Klopp: "It was a good game, a good game, a controlled game in a lot of moments. We deserved the win, 100 per cent, we scored two wonderful goals and we were - in a lot of situations - really dangerous, on the right side especially with Mo, Hendo and Trent, the crosses and the passes. Overall, a really good performance. They had a bit too many set-pieces because they are really good in that and you don't want to give them away, but that's how it is - they go for it as well and we defended them well. All good, 2-0, the game is still on, we have to go there, we have to fight. Porto will try everything to strike back - and that will be a really tough game again, but that's how it should be in the quarter-finals. We will be ready."

Jordan Henderson: "I think we've got to be pleased with the 2-0. There were some good moments in the game [but] obviously we can do better. 2-0, clean sheet - that's important. Obviously we wanted to come out in the second half and score one or two more if we could, but that wasn't the case."

Virgil Van Dijk: "We kept a clean sheet and scored two good goals. We can definitely build on that. You want to enjoy these things and we got a good result today."

MATCH STATS

LIVERPOOL		PORTO
2	GOALS	0
14	ATTEMPTS	9
59%	POSSESSION	41%
4	CORNERS	5
4	OFFSIDES	2
84%	PASSING ACCURACY	71%
107.5KM	DISTANCE COVERED	109.3KM

QUARTER-FINAL 2ND LEG
PORTO V LIVERPOOL

VENUE: Estadio Da Dragao, Porto

DATE: Wednesday 17 April 2019

ATTENDANCE: 49,117

REFEREE: Danny Makkelie (Holland)

RESULT:
Porto 1
Liverpool 4
(agg: 1-6)

GOALS
0-1 Mané '26
0-2 Salah '65
1-2 Eder Militao '68
1-3 Firmino '77
1-4 Van Dijk '84

PORTO: Iker Casillas, Eder Militao, Pepe, Felipe, Alex Telles, Otavio (Tiquinho Soares '46), Danilo Pereira, Hector Herrera, Jesus Manuel Corona (Fernando Andrade dos Santos '78), Moussa Marega, Yacine Brahimi (Bruno Costa '81).

LIVERPOOL: Alisson Becker, Virgil Van Dijk, Andrew Robertson (Jordan Henderson 71'), Joel Matip, Trent Alexander-Arnold (Joe Gomez 66'), Fabinho Tavarez, Georginio Wijnaldum, James Milner, Sadio Mané, Mohamed Salah, Divock Origi (Roberto Firmino 46').

MATCH OVERVIEW

Liverpool eased into the last four of the competition with another emphatic victory away to Porto. The performance may not have hit the heights of the previous season, when the hosts were vanquished 5-0, but once VAR ruled in Mané's favour by allowing his 26th minute goal to stand, the tie was all but over as a contest. Salah made it 2-0 after the break and although Porto responded quickly to pull a goal back it was ultimately to no avail. Firmino came off the bench to score a third and Van Dijk headed home to complete the scoring six minutes from time, setting up a semi-final against Barcelona and a reunion with former Reds Luiz Suarez and Philippe Coutinho.

POST-MATCH REACTION

Jürgen Klopp: "Tonight, they made our life very difficult, they were really direct. It was so powerful the game of Porto and so difficult to deal with, but we scored the goals and that's how a result like this can happen. We have our strengths even in a difficult game, so I am completely happy. It is only important you go through and we went through. Unbelievable. What a competition. We're in the semi-finals for the second time in a row, crazy."

Sergio Conceicao (Porto coach): "Liverpool only had four shots on goal and scored four goals which demonstrates the quality of their team. Today we knew it was possible, we prepared a strategy that I think was appropriate, and at first we did well at all levels. The one time our opponents entered our penalty area, it was a goal. Liverpool are a very strong team."

Jordan Henderson: "I thought the scoreline flattered us a little bit. It was tough, but that's what we expected. Porto make it tough and we dug in from the start. They had some half-chances and it was difficult for the lads but we dug in and we know we can always score."

MATCH STATS

PORTO		LIVERPOOL
1	GOALS	4
20	ATTEMPTS	11
52%	POSSESSION	48%
6	CORNERS	3
2	OFFSIDES	2
78%	PASSING ACCURACY	78%
108.9KM	DISTANCE COVERED	112.3KM

THERE ARE PLACES I REMEMBER...

ISTANBUL 2005

THE MIRACLE OF ISTANBUL

Liverpool pulled off the most miraculous of comebacks to reclaim their mantle as Kings of Europe on a night of unsurpassable drama at the Ataturk Stadium in Istanbul.

Over 40,000 Liverpudlians had made the arduous trek to Turkey to witness their team's long-awaited return to the final of Europe's most coveted cup competition but at half-time they feared the worst.

A first minute goal from Paolo Maldini and two from Hernan Crespo fired AC Milan into an emphatic 3-0 lead and left Liverpool staring into the abyss.

VENUE: Ataturk Stadium, Istanbul

DATE: 25 May 2005

ATTENDANCE: 72,059

RESULT:
Liverpool 3
AC Milan 3
(Liverpool win 3-2 on penalties)

GOALS
Maldini (0-1 '1),
Crespo (0-2 '39),
Crespo (0-3 '44),
Gerrard (1-3 '54),
Smicer (2-3 '56),
Alonso (3-3 '59)

LIVERPOOL:
Dudek, Finnan (Hamann '46), Traore, Riise, Hyypia, Carragher, Alonso, Gerrard, Garcia, Kewell (Smicer '23), Baros (Cisse '85).

AC MILAN: Dida, Cafu, Maldini, Stam, Nesta, Pirlo, Gattuso (Costa '112), Seedorf (Serginho '85), Kaka, Crespo (Tomasson '85), Shevchenko.

A rousing rendition of 'You'll Never Walk Alone' helped lift flagging spirits and what followed was almost beyond belief.

Steven Gerrard's glancing header in the 54th minute was greeted as little more than a consolation but when Vladimir Smicer then struck a long-range effort past Dida two minutes later, a renewed wave of hope rung around the ground.

In the 59th minute Xabi Alonso sensationally scored on the rebound after his penalty had been saved and the fight-back was complete.

A stunning late double save from Jerzy Dudek denied Shevchenko a certain winner and a penalty shoot-out would once again decide the destiny of the trophy.

Amid an unbearable air of tension Dietmar Hamann, Djibril Cisse and Smicer kept their cool to score. John Arne Riise's effort was saved but Serginho blazed over and Dudek saved from both Pirlo and Shevchenko to spark ecstatic scenes.

Liverpool were Champions of Europe for a fifth time and 'Old Big Ears' was on its way back to Anfield for good.

SEMI-FINAL 1ST LEG
BARCELONA V LIVERPOOL

MATCH OVERVIEW

Liverpool's Champions League aspirations were left hanging by a thread after this heavy defeat in Catalonia, even though the end result was never a true reflection of the game. Despite ex-Reds striker Suarez breaking the deadlock midway through the first-half, Liverpool were in the ascendancy for long periods. Failure to convert a succession of chances and the brilliance of Messi, however, eventually conspired to inflict what ended up being the club's joint-heaviest Champions League defeat. Although there was a touch of luck surrounding Barca's second goal, there were no complaints about the stunning free-kick that made it 3-0. Things could have been worse had Dembele not missed a gilt-edged opportunity to score a fourth in injury time, although that seemed to matter little at the time, as Liverpool were still left facing the steepest of uphill tasks.

VENUE: Camp Nou, Barcelona

DATE: Wednesday 1 May 2019

ATTENDANCE: 98,299

REFEREE: Bjorn Kuipers (Holland)

RESULT:
Barcelona 3
Liverpool 0

GOALS
1-0 Suarez '26
2-0 Messi '75
3-0 Messi '82

BARCELONA: Marc-Andre ter Stegen, Sergi Roberto (Carles Alena '90), Gerard Pique, Clement Lenglet, Jordi Alba, Arturo Vidal, Ivan Rakitic, Sergio Busquets, Philippe Coutinho (Nelson Semedo '60), Lionel Messi, Luis Suarez (Ousmane Dembele '90).

LIVERPOOL: Alisson Becker, Virgil Van Dijk, Joe Gomez, Andrew Robertson, Joel Matip, Fabinho Tavarez, Georginio Wijnaldum (Roberto Firmino '78), James Milner (Divock Origi '84), Naby Keïta (Jordan Henderson '24), Sadio Mané, Mohamed Salah.

POST-MATCH REACTION

Jürgen Klopp: "It was a hard result but we have to accept it. I don't know if we can play much better. I think it was the best away game in the Champions League - not only this year, last year included. I told the boys I'm proud of how we played. Against a side like this, playing this kind of football, I was completely happy. I can work really well with this game. I will use this game to show the boys what is possible. It was a brave performance that was very passionate, very lively and, in a lot of moments, creative and direct. Football is like this. It's about scoring goals, and they scored three and we scored none. 3-0 is not the easiest result but we have another game and our people will be there."

Ernesto Valverde (Barcelona coach): "Sometimes you can dominate the rhythm of the game and sometimes they can dominate you. At some moments, Liverpool played the game how they wanted to. It is a great result, but last year we also had an advantage of three goals and well, something happened to us."

Lionel Messi: "It would have been better going to Anfield with a four-goal advantage but this is a terrific result. We got drawn into Liverpool's high-tempo, pretty physical style of play. We aren't used to not owning possession, so this game cost us a little more."

James Milner: "It's tough to take but we need to regroup and take the positives. We'll see what happens and give it everything we've got. Special things have happened at Anfield before."

MATCH STATS

BARCELONA		LIVERPOOL
	GOALS	0
3	ATTEMPTS	14
11	POSSESSION	52%
48%	CORNERS	5
3	OFFSIDES	1
2	PASSING ACCURACY	81%
84%	DISTANCE COVERED	111.1KM
109.7KM		

SEMI-FINAL 2ND LEG
LIVERPOOL V BARCELONA

VENUE: Anfield

DATE: Tuesday 7 May 2019

ATTENDANCE: 52,212

REFEREE: Cuneyt Cakır (Turkey)

RESULT:
Liverpool 4
Barcelona 0
(agg: 4-3)

GOALS
1-0 Origi '7
2-0 Wijnaldum '54
3-0 Wijnaldum '56
4-0 Origi '79

LIVERPOOL: Alisson Becker, Virgil Van Dijk, Andrew Robertson (Georginio Wijnaldum '46), Joel Matip, Trent Alexander-Arnold, Fabinho Tavarez, James Milner, Jordan Henderson, Xherdan Shaqiri (Daniel Sturridge '90), Sadio Mané, Divock Origi (Joe Gomez '85).

BARCELONA: Marc-Andre ter Stegen, Sergi Roberto, Gerard Pique, Clement Lenglet, Jordi Alba, Ivan Rakitic (Malcom '80), Sergio Busquets, Arturo Vidal (Arthur Melo '75), Philippe Coutinho (Nelson Semedo '60), Lionel Messi, Luis Suarez.

MATCH OVERVIEW

On a night that must surely rank as Anfield's greatest, Liverpool defied the longest of odds to pull off what so many had deemed to be impossible. With a 3-0 first leg deficit to overturn, another gallant Champions League campaign looked all but over. To make matters worse, Salah and Firmino were ruled out through injury. Still, there always remained a slight glimmer of hope and when Origi netted, after just seven minutes, that hope turned to belief. Noise levels were cranked up a notch and the Barca superstars appeared shell-shocked. A rampant red tide continued to swarm all over the opposition and when substitute Wijnaldum struck twice in a frenzied three-minute spell they visibly began to wilt. With momentum firmly on Liverpool's side it then came as no surprise when Origi fired home to complete the most heroic of comebacks. Anfield erupted in scenes of wild celebration and another shot at European glory beckoned.

POST-MATCH REACTION

Jürgen Klopp: "It's a special night, very special. Winning against Barcelona is obviously one of the most difficult things in the world of football. We know this club is the mix of atmosphere, emotion, desire and football quality. Cut off one and it doesn't work – we know that. I've said it before. If I have to describe this club then it's a big heart and tonight it was obviously like crazy, pounding like crazy. You could hear it and probably feel it all over the world. I'm so happy we could give the people this experience and I'm really happy about having another chance to get things right from our point of view."

Ernesto Valverde (Barcelona coach): "It's a terrible result for our fans and for ourselves. It's really, really unfortunate, but credit to Liverpool. Things got on top of us after those two quick goals. We didn't manage to get on the scoresheet and they rolled us over really. They surprised us with the fourth goal - presumably my players weren't looking. Liverpool were street smart and they scored."

Georginio Wijnaldum: "Unbelievable. After the game in Spain we were confident we could score four and win 4-0. People outside doubted us and thought we couldn't do it. But once again we showed everything is possible in football."

Luis Suarez: "We have to be ready for all the criticism that is going to rain down on us now. We are very sad, we are in a lot of pain."

MATCH STATS

LIVERPOOL		BARCELONA
4	GOALS	0
13	ATTEMPTS	8
45%	POSSESSION	55%
7	CORNERS	6
1	OFFSIDES	2
76%	PASSING ACCURACY	82%
112.1KM	DISTANCE COVERED	105.4KM

BACK FROM THE BRINK –
HOW BARCA WERE BEATEN

Liverpool's Champions League semi-final second leg victory over Barcelona will be talked about for decades to come but what was it like to play in this amazing game? Here's the inside story of Anfield's greatest-ever comeback, as told by four of the key players involved on that never-to-be-forgotten night...

Virgil Van Dijk: "We had to believe. And I did. One hundred per cent."

Jordan Henderson: "The manager spoke to us before the second leg. He started with the line that the task ahead is normally impossible but because it's us there's a chance we can do something special."

Trent Alexander-Arnold: "If we're being brutally honest, we knew there was only a very, very slim chance of anything happening, but we always knew that the fans would be there for us."

Divock Origi: "The day of the Barcelona game I felt at peace. I had a feeling we could do it."

TAA: "And from the start we battered them."

7 minutes GOAL 1-0!
Henderson surges into the area. His shot is saved by Ter Stegen but Origi is on hand to sweep in the rebound from close range.

JH: "I probably should have scored. I tried to slot it in the bottom corner but the keeper saved it. Thankfully Divock was there for the tap-in."

DO: "The ball came right to my feet and it was just about putting it into the net."

JH: "From that moment, the lads did believe that we had a chance."

54 minutes GOAL 2-0!
Wijnaldum drills Alexander-Arnold's low ball beyond Ter Stegen from 15 yards out.

TAA: "I just tried to pick someone out in the box. It took a decent deflection, ran into the path of Gini and he finished really nice. I think at the moment everyone really started to believe and it gave us a lot of momentum going into the next few minutes."

56 minutes GOAL 3-0!
Wijnaldum, again. This time he rises highest to plant a header from Shaqiri's cross beyond Ter Stegen.

JH: "Obviously, we were delighted with the goals but we knew there was still a lot of time left in the game so we needed to be focused; we needed to defend properly with everything and manage to find one more goal."

79 minutes GOAL 4-0! Alexander-Arnold takes a quick corner and picks out Origi who slams the ball first time into the far corner of the Kop net.

TAA: "Shaq shouted me and said he wanted to take it. As he's walking over and I'm walking away from the ball I've looked across into the box and seen Divock."

DO: "I just felt that I should look back to Trent and see if he would do something. He played it with instinct."

TAA: "No-one was looking so hopefully he'd see it and be able to finish it. Luckily it paid off massively for us."

JH: "Trent having the imagination to take the corner so quick in that moment of the game when we needed a goal was amazing really."

TAA: "I was looking at the ref and the linesman and it was one of them where you don't really believe what's actually just happened. You feel like it's too easy. That a goal like that shouldn't happen in the Champions League semi second leg."

DO: "Looking around you could see what it means for us going 4-0. So much emotion."

FULL-TIME

JH: "When the final whistle went. Obviously it was a moment of joy. I think that game, mentally and physically, was very demanding. I try leave everything on the pitch every time I play football so I needed a bit of help to get back up on my feet. It was an amazing feeling."

VVD: "I couldn't believe what was happening that evening. It was something different. It was out of this world. Everyone was shocked. Tears in their eyes. Nobody could really believe it."

DO: "It was one of the most special nights. We were singing together with the fans. It meant a lot to us."

TAA: "That moment at full-time when we were all singing 'You'll Never Walk Alone' with the fans was, for me, one of the best moments I've had. Without the fans football is nothing so it was an incredible moment for us all to say thank you and to celebrate with them."

JH: "The lads had nothing left. We gave everything. Thankfully we got our rewards for it."

VVD: "It was totally deserved. In the end, it wasn't a bad evening."

WE'RE GOING TO MADRID...

Nearly every famous cup run in Liverpool's recent history has been accompanied by a rousing soundtrack and the road to Madrid 2019 was no exception.

In the same way that 'Ring Of Fire' will forever be associated with the Champions League triumph of 2005, 'Allez Allez Allez' was the song that helped roar the Reds on to the 2018 final in Kiev.

Even way back in the seventies and eighties there are certain tunes that remain synonymous with similar escapades on foreign soil.

In 1977, Kopites who made the pilgrimage to witness the club's maiden European Cup triumph did so with the strains of 'We're On Our Way To Roma' ringing in their ears.

The following year they sang along to 'Underneath The Floodlights', a ditty that celebrated the run to a second successive appearance in the final.

Three years later it was 'Scousers In Gay Paree', while in 1984 the intrepid Red travellers returned to the lion's den of Rome chanting 'Campioni Liverpool' as a rebuke to the locals who were prematurely preparing to celebrate victory.

And so to 2019. And a new song that every Liverpool supporter will now be familiar with. Sung to the tune of The Beautiful South's hit record of 1996 'Rotterdam', it tells the story of how Jürgen Klopp's team battled their way through to the Champions League final in Madrid.

It was sung loud and proud during games towards the latter part of the season and could be heard reverberating around the streets of the Spanish capital ahead of the clash with Tottenham at the Estadio Metropolitano.

In case you still don't know the words, it goes like this…

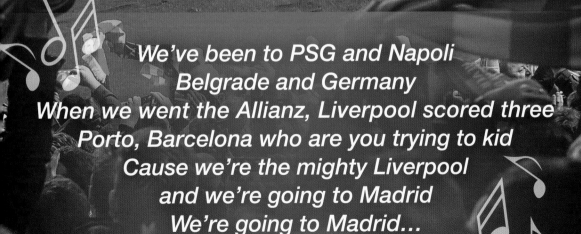

We've been to PSG and Napoli
Belgrade and Germany
When we went the Allianz, Liverpool scored three
Porto, Barcelona who are you trying to kid
Cause we're the mighty Liverpool
and we're going to Madrid
We're going to Madrid…

WELCOME TO 'MAD-RED'

Liverpudlians converged on Madrid in their thousands for the 2019 Champions League final and the party began well in advance of kick-off at the Estadio Metropolitano.

The mass exodus to Spain began as early as the weekend before with all manner of crazy routes planned by supporters desperate to see their team lift number six.

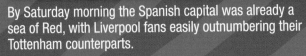

By Saturday morning the Spanish capital was already a sea of Red, with Liverpool fans easily outnumbering their Tottenham counterparts.

It is estimated that between sixty and seventy thousand made the trip and the majority gathered at Madrid's Plaza Felipe II – the designated Fan Park for Liverpool supporters.

Here, they were entertained by DJs and musicians, including John Power of The La's/Cast fame, Timo Tierney of The Tea Street band, Chelcee Grimes and BossNight favourites Ben Burke, Kieran Molyneux and Jamie Webster.

The atmosphere was electric and one of celebration, setting the tone for the unforgettable night that lay ahead…

ESTADIO METROPOLITANO: A BRIEF HISTORY

- Estadio Metropolitano is the home of Atletico Madrid and has been since the start of the 2017/18 season.

- The current stadium was originally built in the early 1990s (1990-93) as part of Madrid's unsuccessful bid to host the 1997 World Athletic Championships and officially opened on 6 September 1994.

- Previously it was known as Estadio de la Comunidad (Madrid Community Stadium) and Estadio Olimpico de Madrid (Madrid Olympic Stadium) but was more commonly referred to as Estadio de La Peineta (The Comb Stadium).

- It closed in 2004 and Atletico took ownership of the site in 2013, carrying out renovations at a cost of 240 million euros ahead of their eventual move from the Vincente Calderon.

- Naming rights for the stadium were acquired by the Wanda Group, a Chinese real estate company.

- In September 2017 it was awarded the honour of staging this Champions League final, beating off competition from the Baku National Stadium in Azerbaijan.

- It is the 31st different venue to stage a European Cup/Champions League final.

- And the fifth to be held in Madrid, with all previous finals in the Spanish capital being played at the Bernabeu.

- Previous finals in Madrid…

1957 – Real Madrid v Fiorentina
1969 – AC Milan v Ajax
1980 – Nottingham Forest v Hamburg
2010 – Inter Milan v Bayern Munich

- The only city to have staged more European Cup/Champions League finals than Madrid is London, with seven (all at Wembley).

- Estadio Metropolitano is ranked as a four-star stadium by UEFA, with a capacity of 67,829.

- The record attendance of 67,804 was set on 9 February 2019 when Atletico took on Real Madrid in La Liga.

- In March 2018 it hosted international football for the first time when Spain played Argentina.

- The following month it was the chosen venue for the Copa del Rey final between Sevilla and Barcelona.

CHAMPIONS LEAGUE FINAL 2019

UEFA CHAMPIONS LEAGUE

VENUE:
Estadio Wanda Metropolitano, Madrid (Spain)

DATE:
Saturday
1 June 2019

ATTENDANCE:
63,272

REFEREE:
Damir Skomina
(Slovenia)

ASSISTANT REFEREES:
Jure Praprotnik (Slovenia) & Robert Vukan (Slovenia)

LIVERPOOL:
13. Alisson Becker
4. Virgil Van Dijk
26. Andrew Robertson
32. Joel Matip
66. Trent Alexander-Arnold
3. Fabinho Tavarez
5. Georginio Wijnaldum
14. Jordan Henderson
9. Roberto Firmino
10. Sadio Mané
11. Mohamed Salah

SUBSTITUTES
27. Divock Origi
(on for Firmino '58)
7. James Milner
(on for Wijnaldum '62)
12. Joe Gomez
(on for Mané '90)

TOTTENHAM HOTSPUR
1. Hugo Lloris
2. Kieran Trippier
4. Toby Alderweireld
5. Jan Vertonghen
3. Danny Rose
17. Moussa Sissoko
8. Harry Winks
23. Christian Eriksen
20. Deli Alli
7. Heung-min Son
10. Harry Kane

SUBSTITUTES
27. Lucas Moura
(on for Winks '66)
15. Eric Dier
(on for Sissoko '74)
18. Fernando Llorente
(on for Alli '82)

YOU'LL NEVER WALK ALONE

As the Liverpool players emerged from the tunnel of the Estadio Metropolitano in Madrid, a quick glance to their right would have made them feel instantly at home.

For it was at this end of the ground that the majority of travelling Reds were housed.

And the team's '12th Man' certainly put on a spectacle to behold.

Armed with their usual vast array of flags and banners, they were in full voice throughout and yet again would have a key role to play on a momentous occasion in Liverpool's history...

IN SUNNY SPAIN WE WON IT SIX TIMES

It won't be remembered as the greatest Champions League final of all-time but who cares? An early Mo Salah penalty and late Divock Origi strike were enough to settle this all-English clash in the Spanish capital and clinch a sixth European crown for Liverpool. Relive the key moments as they happened…

01 min: PENALTY! Mané's cross into the Tottenham box is handled by Sissoko and the referee immediately points to the spot.

02 mins: GOAL! Salah gives Liverpool a dream start by driving home the resultant spot-kick. 1-0.

10 mins: Sissoko shoots high and wide with a speculative effort from outside the box.

17 mins: Alexander-Arnold goes close with a long-range effort that skims narrowly past the far post.

20 mins: Son finds space behind the Liverpool defence but is thwarted by a timely challenge from Alexander-Arnold.

22 mins: Salah shoots to the left of goal from inside the Tottenham area.

33 mins: Matip makes a vital block to prevent Sissoko sending Son clean through on goal.

34 mins: Matip is being kept busy at the back and is on hand with another important interception, this time to deny Alli.

38 mins: Robertson embarks on a surging 70-yard run down the left side that results in him unleashing a shot that Lloris tips over.

39 mins: Salah tries his luck from outside the box following the resultant corner, his attempt goes way over.

43 mins: As the interval approaches Liverpool force a succession of corners but Tottenham cope comfortably with the danger.

45 mins: The last action of the first half sees Eriksen fire over from 20-yards.

HALF-TIME – TOTTEHAM 0-1 LIVERPOOL

47 mins: Tottenham begin the second-half strongly but Kane's cross is scrambled away.

53 mins: Fabinho tries his luck from distance only to see his effort fall comfortably into the arms of Lloris after taking a deflection off Winks.

54 mins: Liverpool maintain the pressure. Salah has a shot blocked and Robertson's cross is then cut out by Lloris.

57 mins: A Tottenham corner is punched clear by Alisson and Salah then blocks the follow-up by Rose.

58 mins: The first substitution of the evening sees Firmino replaced by Origi.

62 mins: Klopp makes his second change, sending Milner on at the expense of Wijnaldum.

65 mins: Pochettino responds by replacing Winks with Moura.

69 mins: Milner goes close to scoring with a low strike that rolls narrowly past the post.

73 mins: Alli attempts to lob Alisson but the Liverpool keeper is alert to the danger and handles it with ease.

74 mins: Tottenham make their second substitution, with Dier coming on for Sissoko.

75 mins: Son's attempt to outpace Van Dijk and run through on goal is fruitless as the Reds defender deals with the threat in expert fashion.

79 mins: Alli heads over from a Trippier cross.

80 mins: A double save from Alisson thwarts Son and then Moura.

82 mins: Tottenham make their final change as Alli makes way for Llorente.

85 mins: Liverpool find themselves under pressure but Alisson flings himself across goal to keep out a shot from Eriksen.

88 mins: GOAL! A Liverpool corner from the right ends up at the feet of Origi who drills the ball low into the bottom corner, sparking ecstatic scenes of celebration among the supporters behind the goal. 2-0.

90 mins: As five minutes of stoppage time beckon Liverpool's final substitution is Gomez for Mané.

92 mins: Alisson pushes a shot from Son around the post.

FULL-TIME
TOTTENHAM 0
LIVERPOOL 2

LIVERPOOL ARE CHAMPIONS OF EUROPE!

1-0

2-0

71

All the need-to-know facts and figures from the 2019 Champions League final...

- The 2019 Champions League final was the first time Liverpool had ever played a competitive match in the month of June.

- It was also the first Champions League final in history not to feature a yellow or red card for either side.

- And the first in which 12 substitutes were permitted to be named on the bench.

- Jürgen Klopp has guided Liverpool to a final in every one of his three European campaigns as manager of the Reds, meaning he is yet to lose a two-legged tie since coming to England.

- Only Bob Paisley has taken Liverpool to more European finals than Jürgen Klopp.

- Roberto Firmino and James Milner are the only players to have featured in each of those three finals, with Firmino the only one to have started in them all.

- The eleven players selected by Klopp for the Champions League final had never started a game together before.

- Trent Alexander-Arnold was the youngest player in Liverpool's Champions League winning team but also the most experienced defender. This was his 23rd European appearance for the Reds, five ahead of Van Dijk and Robertson.

- At the age of 20 years and 237 days, Alexander-Arnold also became the first player under the age of 21 to start successive Champions League finals.

- And he is the club's youngest-ever European Cup winner, excluding unused substitutes.

- Andy Robertson is the first Scotsman to win the Champions League since Paul Lambert did so with Borussia Dortmund in 1997.

- Mo Salah's penalty – timed at 01:48 – was the second quickest goal in a Champions League final. The record for the fastest belongs to Paolo Maldini who scored against Liverpool in 2005 after just 50 seconds.

- Salah converted the penalty with his first touch of the ball.

- Alisson Becker, Trent Alexander-Arnold, Andy Robertson and Roberto Firmino had not yet touched the ball when Liverpool went one up.

- Joel Matip's first ever assist in a Liverpool shirt was for the ball he played to Divock Origi, from which the winning goal was scored.

- During the course of the 2018/19 Champions League campaign Origi had just three shots on goal and scored with every one of them.

- Only two players featured in every Champions League game for Liverpool in 2018/19 – Sadio Mané and Alisson Becker, with the latter playing every minute.

- Mo Salah was Liverpool's top scorer in the competition with five goals.

- Virgil Van Dijk was named as UEFA's official man-of-the-match in the final, emulating the achievement of Steven Gerrard who won it in 2005.

- Liverpool were well represented in the 20-man UEFA Champions League Squad of the Season, with Alisson Becker, Virgil Van Dijk, Trent Alexander-Arnold, Andy Robertson, Georginio Wijnaldum and Sadio Mané all selected.

- Three different players captained the Reds during the 2018/19 Champions League – Jordan Henderson (6), James Milner (4) and Virgil Van Dijk (1).

- Henderson became the fifth Liverpool skipper to lift the trophy, following in the footsteps of Emlyn Hughes (twice), Phil Thompson, Graeme Souness and Steven Gerrard.

- The 2019 Champions League is Liverpool's first major honour since the 2012 League Cup.

- Victory in Madrid ended a run of six successive final defeats for Jürgen Klopp, three with Liverpool (League Cup, Europa League and Champions League) and three with Borussia Dortmund (German Cup twice & Champions League).

- Klopp is the fifth German manager to win the European Cup but only the second (after Jupp Heynckes) to win it with a non-German team.

- Liverpool's six European Cup triumphs have come against teams playing in all-white.

- And this 2-0 win was the first time Liverpool had won the cup by a margin of more than one goal since the 3-1 win over Borussia Moenchengladbach in 1977.

- Liverpool have now extended their position as English football's most successful club in European competition, taking their tally of trophies won to 12 (six European Cup/Champions Leagues, three UEFA Cups, three Super Cups).

- Their collection of six European Cups is double that of their nearest challengers Manchester United and they are now outright third in the overall list of European Cup winners, behind only AC Milan (7) and Real Madrid (13).

MATCH STATS

TOTTENHAM		LIVERPOOL
0	GOALS	2
16	ATTEMPTS	14
8	ATTEMPTS ON TARGET	3
5	ATTEMPTS OFF TARGET	5
3	BLOCKED	6
1	SAVES	8
8	CORNERS	9
3	OFFSIDES	2
5	FOULS COMMITTED	6
5	FOULS SUFFERED	3
30	BALLS RECOVERED	37
1	TACKLES	1
6	BLOCKS	3
17	CLEARANCES	23
61%	POSSESSION	39%
528	PASSES	280
428	PASSES COMPLETED	189
81%	PASSING ACCURACY	68%
103.4KM	DISTANCE COVERED	105.1KM

WE ARE THE CHAMPIONS!

UEFA CHAMPIONS LEAGUE®

How does it feel to be a Champions League winner? Here's how the Liverpool squad reacted after the match...

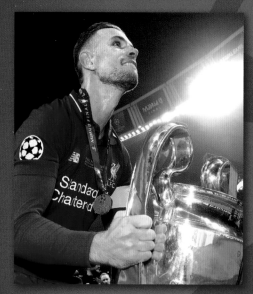

Mohamed Salah: "Everybody is happy now! I'm very glad to play the second final in a row and the full 90 minutes, finally. It wasn't a good performance from any of us individually but that doesn't matter now."

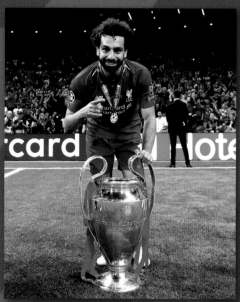

Jordan Henderson: "Without this manager, this is impossible. You go through tough times in a season, but what he has done since coming in is unbelievable. Not only the players he's brought in that have made us stronger, but he's also made the players who were already here better. There's such a togetherness, he has created a special dressing room - all the praise goes to the manager. I'm so proud to be a part of this football club and to cap it with this is so special to me. I've had tough times but I've kept going - just as this club has. It's the best moment of my life apart from [having] my children, this is what I dreamed of since I was a kid. It's not about me, it's not about me being captain or lifting the trophy, it's about this club, these players, this manager. Now we must keep going and kick on."

Sadio Mané: "It was a long way to go, but we finally did it together. It was not easy, but that's what makes people love football. We are very proud and very happy to win this trophy. The dream has come true. I could not have anything better. I can't describe how good Alisson was - I saw him make incredible saves for us. We are very happy to have him in our squad. He makes us even better. For me he is the best in the world. We have more things to come. We will do everything to win [more] trophies with this squad."

Trent Alexander-Arnold: "It's hard to even put into words what's just happened. With the season we've had, we deserved it more than any other team. We've beaten everyone put in our path and we have done something special again tonight. We were probably dominated for the main part of the game but we showed we're a world class side and can win anyway. When we look back tonight we're not going to think it was a sluggish game, we're going to think we've just won the European Cup! I'm just a normal lad from Liverpool whose dream just came true."

James Milner: "It will be nice going to Melwood and seeing number six there. When I signed for the club I was desperate to add trophies as this club expects to win trophies. It has an amazing history but we want to create our own history. We have started that and put a trophy on the board. We did not play well but a cup final is all about getting the result. It was a tough game. Sometimes scoring early is great, but the scoreboard can knock you out of your stride. There was a lot of tired people out there. There was a lot of emotion. Last year helped us, and the Europa League final before that. It helps when you have been there before and we have done it."

Joel Matip: "I know it's one of the biggest games, but I just wanted to enjoy that I had the opportunity. It's the kind of game you want to play as a kid. It's really good that we've had so many wins this season. It's hard to compare different parts of my career, but I am really enjoying the time now and, of course, winning the Champions League is an incredible feeling."

Andy Robertson: "I haven't often seen my dad cry, but he hasn't stopped since the final whistle. I am lost for words. It's an unbelievable achievement and I don't think it will sink in for a long time. I believed it was possible, but it was all about how we used the disappointment of getting beat in the final [last year]. Luckily, we used it to our advantage. We used that as motivation. We needed to try and get the Champions League trophy because we feel that [with] everything we've put in this season, it was amazing to cap it off like that. The way the fans have conducted themselves, as well, this season, they deserved a trophy after the disappointment of last season and obviously the last day of this [Premier League] season. We hoped we could do that for them and the club."

Georginio Wijnaldum: "We are still in a moment where we have to realise that we have just won the Champions League. What a season we had. It's good that we finished it with a medal. We played better games this season, but at the end it doesn't matter if you win the game. We could have done better but I prefer not to play well and to win the game, because they played quite well and didn't win it. That's what we learned during the years. Let's hope that this is just the beginning because that means we still can win titles. If this is the beginning, it's a good beginning and hopefully more [trophies] will follow. Next, hopefully, we can win the Premier League."

Divock Origi: "We done it. First, it's about the team but I'm happy I could play my part. It's unbelievable. Winning a Champions League is so hard. Today we're here, we pulled together with the team and supporters and we have to celebrate all together. I think we just did it as a team, we made a positive step forward. We kept improving ourselves and we used the experiences of the past for now. We have a good mix of talent and experienced players and today was just about enjoying it and we did."

Jürgen Klopp was, not surprisingly, a man in demand in the immediate aftermath of the 2019 Champions League final. This was the manager's post-match verdict…

On what was different about this final compared to Kiev the year before…

"The result, obviously. We all spoke about it a lot, I played many more finals than I won, we always played better football. Tonight it was a big challenge for both teams to deal with the three-week [break] because you never have a period with three weeks and no game. So keep the rhythm or get the rhythm back actually. Then obviously it was different circumstances for two English teams, it was pretty warm. You saw it was a fight. A final is about the result and we need to make this experience a little bit longer or more often than others. Tonight the boys showed it, the resilience and everything you need to block the decisive balls.

Ali [Alisson] had to make a few saves, he, of course, played a sensational game, absolutely, he looked completely unbeatable, pretty much. That helped us. [We] scored goals in the right moment. Usually I always sit here a bit earlier and have to explain how you can lose this game. This time, I don't want to explain why we won it, I only want to enjoy that we won it. All the rest is not important. It's for all the people around the world, in the stadium, they are with us and now celebrating like crazy. Whoever is in Liverpool tomorrow we will celebrate together and we will have a sensational night.

I feel mostly relief, to be honest, relief for my family, actually, because they are pretty close to me and the last six times we always flew on holiday with a silver medal, that doesn't feel too cool. This is completely different this year. It's for them as well, that's great. It's for the supporters of course, but for our owners as well because they never put real pressure on us, they appreciate the development, they see the steps we make. It's for them as well. For the players, we were all pretty much crying on the pitch because it was so emotional, it was so big, it means so much to us.

On the other hand and I should have probably said this first of all, I know how Tottenham feel in this moment better than anybody else in the world. They played a sensational season as well and they would have deserved it as well, but tonight we scored the goals in the right moment. I told Poch already after the game that he should be really proud of what they did this year as well."

On what is the most satisfying thing about the achievement…

"I'm happy for the boys. You know what people said about a couple of players of this team. Jordan Henderson is captain of the Champions League winner 2019 – that's satisfying actually. That Millie did it at the age of 33. They are all very important. But I can say again, without Millie's dressing-room talks before the game – with a non-native manager – I think it would not be possible. It's so important.

All the things they did during the weeks, how they lifted when we had little downs, it's just incredible. Tonight is really emotional, that's my main feeling, it's overwhelming, all that stuff. It feels really good but I'm much calmer than I thought I would be when it finally happened. It was not important to me to touch the cup or whatever. I loved the pictures when the boys had it, I loved it when I saw a few faces in the stands. That gave me everything I need. Tomorrow, going to Liverpool and having something to celebrate, that's big and I'm really looking forward to that."

On what this means to him personally…

"We spoke two days ago about my 'unlucky' career, somehow. When I hear it I think, 'Yeah, people could see it like this', but I don't feel it, to be honest, because I always see the way to a final as well because that's, of course, important for me as well. I think my life is much better than I ever expected it, so winning something is good, it's cool, but it's for all the other people. I'm not so much in it, I'm much more really in development but I get it, we have to win things, so for us it's really important that people don't ask now all the time about not winning or winning things.

Now we won something and we will carry on. We want to win things, 100 per cent. I've

said it, this is only the start for this group. It's still a wonderful age group, they all have the best times in their careers ahead of them so that's big. For me, I'm really happy. I have a lot of silver medals and now I have a golden one so it'll be next to the silver medals in my house and that's cool. But mostly I'm happy for all the other people. When you see it now in the dressing room, everybody feels it but you don't really know what to do with it. But tomorrow I'm really sure when we drive through the city, then we all will realise what these boys have done and that's the best moment, for sure."

On the win being a collective effort…

"Tonight, I am so happy for the players and I'm happy really for my family, and there will be a moment when I'm overwhelmed for myself maybe. But look at my coaches, what we all did during the year to try to make the next step. But it feels so good: 97 points, now you can say it, 97 points in the league is incredible and winning the Champions League – that's an unbelievably long way to go and we did it, that's incredible. But after the final last year, when we came home to Liverpool, it was not cool but one of my friends is a singer and my assistant coach we sang a song: 'We saw the European Cup, Madrid had all the luck, we swear we'll keep on being cool, we'll bring it back to Liverpool.' Nobody thought in that moment it would happen. In that moment it was only to lift our mood a little bit and now it happened actually, so we have to think about what we will sing tonight because obviously it means something."

On next year's final being in Istanbul…

"I told UEFA already: we will be there! Give me a few minutes! We know that sometimes we carry the burden of history and making Istanbul happen again will be a target I would say, but it will be difficult."

MAN OF THE MATCH

Cool, calm and a consistently reassuring presence at the heart of Liverpool's defence, Virgil Van Dijk's first full season in a red shirt has been the stuff dreams are made of and the big Dutchman capped it all with a man-of-the-match performance in the Champions League final...

Virgil what are your views on the game itself?

"We were playing against Spurs so we knew before the game that it was going to be very tough. In the first half, Tottenham didn't create too many chances, at least not big chances, while we did have a couple ourselves. Obviously scoring the penalty in the first minute helps a lot and it gave us a boost. It can also be very dangerous because it's mentally pretty tough in a final, but we dug deep. In the second half they were good, created chances and we had it tough. They were putting pressure on us and with their opportunities they looked a bit dangerous which happens in games. Ali was there to save us with a couple of shots but we prepared for it. We know that there will be moments in games where you are going to have difficulties, but if you are prepared for it, it is easier to deal with and it was all good in the end. I think overall we are deserved Champions League winners."

There was a three-week gap between the end of the Premier League season and the Champions League final, was that a problem for you?

"To be fair, it wasn't any harder than normal. I think it suited us and maybe Tottenham as well. We had a short break of six days off so we had time to get our heads off football and enjoy a bit of a break.

Then after that we had the training camp in Marbella so we got used to the Spanish climate and we were working very hard with double sessions and a friendly game. It was all in preparation for this."

How did it feel to finally get your hands on the trophy?

"It's a beautiful trophy. Last year was very tough and to be able to hold it this year is special. I'm very proud of this group of players, proud of everyone who is involved with Liverpool, everyone who has been a part of this success because this is definitely a success. We wanted to write our own history. We have been working our socks off the whole season, day in day out. Obviously, it was tough not to win the league, but to be able to get the opportunity to win this Champions League – and then to actually do it – was something to give everything for."

Tell us about the influence Jürgen Klopp has had on this Liverpool team...

"He's a fantastic manager first and foremost but a fantastic human being as well. How he handles us players at the games but also outside of games is outstanding. It's a pleasure to work with him but also the rest of the coaching staff and all the people who work at Melwood. It's an amazing environment to be in and I'm very glad and very proud that he wanted me to play for this beautiful club."

Now that you've won your first piece of silverware with Liverpool, are you hungry for more success?

"I think we should be hungry anyway but this season with Liverpool has been good and now we have got the Champions League which is something that we definitely wanted. I think when we start again in July everyone starts anew and everyone is working towards their goals.

Obviously we want to challenge for every trophy if possible. We have the squad for it but you saw this year that you still have to do it. Hopefully we can challenge Man City for the title again next season because I don't think they will go anywhere and nor will we. Being in the Champions League final two years in a row is special and it's something we hope to be in every year but we know how difficult it is to reach it. We're all ambitious and we all want to have those kinds of nights a couple of times a year, so let's just go for it. Work hard and stay humble. That's the only way forward."

How would you like this season to be remembered?

"That we had something to cheer about at the end! Hopefully this is just the start. I think the manager has said it before in interviews. It's not like we tried it this year and next year we're not going to try it anymore. We have a fantastic team, a great age group of players who can play together for hopefully the next four or five years and build on this season. We tried everything until the last opportunity in the Premier League. We did the same in the Champions League and thankfully it was enough."

VVD'S CHAMPIONS LEAGUE FINAL STATS

TOUCHES: 40
PASSES: 32
PASSING ACCURACY: 71.9%
LONG BALLS: 7
ACCURATE LONG BALLS: 3
AERIAL DUELS WON: 3
SHOTS: 1
TACKLES: 1
CLEARANCES: 5
BLOCKS: 1

TURNING THE TOWN RED

This was the day after the momentous night before.

On Sunday 2 June, Liverpool returned home to a breath-taking reception – one that was truly befitting their new status as Kings of Europe.

It was early afternoon when the squad touched down at John Lennon airport, the plane transporting them back from Spain being greeted by a ceremonial water arc – a salute traditionally reserved for visiting foreign dignitaries or military veterans.

Unbeknown to those on board, an estimated three quarters of a million people were lining the streets of Merseyside to hail their heroes.

Jürgen Klopp: "I cannot really describe it because I cried a little bit as well because it's so overwhelming what the people are doing. When you have a direct eye contact and you see how much it means to them that's touching, to be honest. It's brilliant. Thank God the weather changed in a positive direction so we are having a wonderful time here. It's really special. I don't know exactly how many people live in Liverpool but there's not a lot of space for fans and supporters of other clubs, so it's incredible! This team is really doing so well and if you are a young kid, which team would you support? There are not a lot of other options and opportunities apart from Liverpool so it's really nice to see. You see in their eyes how much it means. It's unbelievable and it's so intense. Today, wow! It's crazy."

Some fans had been waiting since early morning, eager to grab the best vantage point for when the open-top bus containing the victorious team passed by.

From Allerton, where the four-hour victory parade commenced, through to Childwall, Broadgreen, West Derby, Tuebrook, Kensington and finally the city centre, the red-painted pavements thronged with jubilant supporters as the celebrations continued.

Jordan Henderson: "It's amazing, absolutely amazing. We were looking forward to it straight after the party last night, to get back. It's amazing to come back with the trophy to show the fans."

Divock Origi: "It feels good. I think today we can celebrate. We have a wonderful team and Liverpool is celebrating today, we can feel it. It means a lot to the people, I can see it in their eyes and in their reaction. It means so much and it's beautiful for us because we give so much on the pitch and whenever you come back and you get a welcome like this it's always good."

Virgil van Dijk: "It's amazing, it's something special. You have to really experience it. It's unbelievable what it does to the city and obviously to the club as well. I'm very proud to be sitting on this coach and hopefully we can have more days like this. I think there's still more to come but it's already been passed my expectations. I'm just taking everything in and enjoying every bit of it with all of these fans."

Such incredible scenes had not been witnessed in these parts since the Reds had last won the Champions League 14 years previous, and the city was partying like it was 2005 all over again.

On rooftops, bus stops and traffic lights, supporters clambered, desperate for a glimpse of the gleaming silver trophy as it shimmered like a diamond among a vast sea of red.

Georginio Wijnaldum: "Amazing. It's difficult to put into words; it's something you have to feel. It's phenomenal. You see how many people come to see the bus tour, it's more than I expected. To see grandmas, grandpas, babies, all kinds of ages - you see how much it means to the city."

Joe Gomez: "It's an amazing feeling to share with all the boys. It's special, seriously. You see all these people: it sums up what it means to play for the club and it's special to be part of history."

Dejan Lovren: "What we did in previous years, unfortunately we lost a couple of finals. But all these people never stopped believing in us. It's a gift to them and they say thank you. It's both ways - incredible."

Peter Krawietz: "It is absolutely unbelievable. There are not a lot of clubs in the world where you can make this - winning titles and having so much togetherness with the team and the fans."

Alisson Becker: "I have no words to explain because I thought it was a great thing just winning the Champions League, but when you are here feeling the emotion of these people, our supporters, it's amazing."

The crowds were at their most dense along the city's symbolic waterfront and here, on the banks of the Mersey, the world-famous Liver Birds looked proudly down, as plumes of red smoke, fireworks and tickertape greeted the arrival of the newly crowned European champions.

The images captured are already iconic.

It was a homecoming that will live long in the memory and the story it told was that LIVERPOOL FOOTBALL CLUB is back on its lofty perch…

UEFA CHAMPIONS LEAGUE 2018/19: ALL THE RESULTS...

MATCHDAY ONE

Group A
Club Brugge 0-1 Borussia Dortmund
Monaco 1-2 Atletico Madrid

Group B
Barcelona 4-0 PSV Eindhoven
Inter 2-1 Tottenham Hotspur

Group C
Liverpool 3-2 Paris Saint-Germain
Red Star Belgrade 0-0 Napoli

Group D
Galatasaray 3-0 Lokomotiv Moscow
Schalke 1-1 Porto

Group E
Ajax 3-0 AEK Athens
Benfica 0-2 Bayern Munich

Group F
Shakhtar 2-2 Hoffenheim
Manchester City 1-2 Lyon

Group G
Real Madrid 3-0 AS Roma
Viktoria Plzen 2-2 CSKA Moscow

Group H
Young Boys 0-3 Manchester United
Valencia 0-2 Juventus

MATCHDAY TWO

Group A
Atletico Madrid 3-1 Club Brugge
Borussia Dortmund 3-0 Monaco

Group B
Tottenham Hotspur 2-4 Barcelona
PSV Eindhoven 1-2 Inter

Group C
Napoli 1-0 Liverpool
Paris Saint-Germain 6-1 Red Star Belgrade

Group D
Lokomotiv Moscow 0-1 Schalke
Porto 1-0 Galatasaray

Group E
Bayern Munich 1-1 Ajax
AEK Athens 2-3 Benfica

Group F
Hoffenheim 1-2 Manchester City
Lyon 2-2 Shakhtar

Group G
CSKA Moscow 1-0 Real Madrid
AS Roma 5-0 Viktoria Plzen

Group H
Juventus 3-0 Young Boys
Manchester United 0-0 Valencia

MATCHDAY THREE

Group A
Club Brugge 1-1 Monaco
Borussia Dortmund 4-0 Atletico Madrid

Group B
PSV Eindhoven 2-2 Tottenham Hotspur
Barcelona 2-0 Inter

Group C
Liverpool 4-0 Red Star Belgrade
Paris Saint-Germain 2-2 Napoli

Group D
Lokomotiv Moscow 1-3 Porto
Galatasaray 0-0 Schalke

Group E
AEK Athens 0-2 Bayern Munich
Ajax 1-0 Benfica

Group F
Hoffenheim 3-3 Lyon
Shakhtar 0-3 Manchester City

Group G
AS Roma 3-0 CSKA Moscow
Real Madrid 2-1 Viktoria Plzen

Group H
Young Boys 1-1 Valencia
Manchester United 0-1 Juventus

MATCHDAY FOUR

Group A
Monaco 0-4 Club Brugge
Atletico Madrid 2-0 Borussia Dortmund

Group B
Tottenham Hotspur 2-1 PSV Eindhoven
Inter 1-1 Barcelona

Group C
Red Star Belgrade 2-0 Liverpool
Napoli 1-1 Paris Saint-Germain

Group D
Porto 4-1 Lokomotiv Moscow
Schalke 2-0 Galatasaray

Group E
Bayern Munich 2-0 AEK Athens
Benfica 1-1 Ajax

Group F
Lyon 2-2 Hoffenheim
Manchester City 6-0 Shakhtar

Group G
CSKA Moscow 1-2 Roma
Viktoria Plzen 0-5 Real Madrid

Group H
Valencia 3-1 Young Boys
Juventus 1-2 Manchester United

MATCHDAY FIVE

Group A
Atletico Madrid 2-0 Monaco
Borussia Dortmund 0-0 Club Brugge

Group B
PSV Eindhoven 1-2 Barcelona
Tottenham Hotspur 1-0 Inter

Group C
Paris Saint-Germain 2-1 Liverpool
Napoli 3-1 Red Star Belgrade

Group D
Lokomotiv Moscow 2-0 Galatasaray
Porto 3-1 Schalke

Group E
AEK Athens 0-2 Ajax
Bayern Munich 5-1 Benfica

Group F
Hoffenheim 2-3 Shakhtar
Lyon 2-2 Manchester City

Group G
CSKA Moscow 1-2 Viktoria Plzen
AS Roma 0-2 Real Madrid

Group H
Manchester United 1-0 Young Boys
Juventus 1-0 Valencia

MATCHDAY SIX

Group A
Club Brugge 0-0 Atletico Madrid
Monaco 0-2 Borussia Dortmund

Group B
Barcelona 1-1 Tottenham Hotspur
Inter 1-1 PSV Eindhoven

Group C
Liverpool 1-0 Napoli
Red Star Belgrade 1-4 Paris Saint-Germain

Group D
Galatasaray 2-3 Porto
Schalke 1-0 Lokomotiv Moscow

Group E
Ajax 3-3 Bayern Munich
Benfica 1-0 AEK Athens

Group F
Shakhtar 1-1 Lyon
Manchester City 2-1 Hoffenheim

Group G
Real Madrid 0-3 CSKA Moscow
Viktoria Plzen 2-1 AS Roma

Group H
Young Boys 2-1 Juventus
Valencia 2-1 Manchester United

FINAL GROUP TABLES

Group A		P	W	D	L	F	A	Pts
1.	Borussia Dortmund	6	4	1	1	10	2	13
2.	Atletico Madrid	6	4	1	1	9	6	13
3.	Club Brugge	6	1	3	2	6	5	6
4.	AS Monaco	6	0	1	5	2	14	1

Group B		P	W	D	L	F	A	Pts
1.	FC Barcelona	6	4	2	0	14	5	14
2.	Tottenham Hotspur	6	2	2	2	9	10	8
3.	Inter Milan	6	2	2	2	6	7	8
4.	PSV Eindhoven	6	0	2	4	6	13	2

Group C		P	W	D	L	F	A	Pts
1.	PSG	6	3	2	1	17	9	11
2.	Liverpool	6	3	0	3	9	7	9
3.	Napoli	6	2	3	1	7	5	9
4.	Red Star Belgrade	6	1	1	4	5	17	4

Group D		P	W	D	L	F	A	Pts
1.	Porto	6	5	1	0	15	6	16
2.	Schalke 04	6	3	2	1	6	4	11
3.	Galatasaray	6	1	1	4	5	8	4
4.	Lokomotiv Moscow	6	1	0	5	4	12	3

Group E		P	W	D	L	F	A	Pts
1.	Bayern Munich	6	4	2	0	15	5	14
2.	Ajax	6	3	3	0	11	5	12
3.	Benfica	6	2	1	3	6	11	7
4.	AEK Athens	6	0	0	6	2	13	0

Group F		P	W	D	L	F	A	Pts
1.	Man City	6	4	1	1	16	6	13
2.	Lyon	6	1	5	0	12	11	8
3.	Shakhtar Donetsk	6	1	3	2	8	16	6
4.	TSG 1899 Hoffenheim	6	0	3	3	11	14	3

Group G		P	W	D	L	F	A	Pts
1.	Real Madrid	6	4	0	2	12	5	12
2.	AS Roma	6	3	0	3	11	8	9
3.	Viktoria Plzen	6	2	1	3	7	16	7
4.	CSKA Moscow	6	2	1	3	8	9	7

Group H		P	W	D	L	F	A	Pts
1.	Juventus	6	4	0	2	9	4	12
2.	Man United	6	3	1	2	7	4	10
3.	Valencia	6	2	2	2	6	6	8
4.	Young Boys	6	1	1	4	4	12	4

Round of 16 1st leg

Manchester United 0-2 Paris Saint-Germain
AS Roma 2-1 Porto
Tottenham Hotspur 3-0 Borussia Dortmund
Ajax 1-2 Real Madrid
Liverpool 0-0 Bayern Munich
Lyon 0-0 Barcelona
Schalke 2-3 Manchester City
Atletico Madrid 2-0 Juventus

Round of 16 2nd leg

Borussia Dortmund 0-1 Tottenham Hotspur (agg: 0-4)
Real Madrid 1-4 Ajax (agg: 3-5)
Paris Saint-Germain 1-3 Manchester United (agg: 3-3, United win on away goals)
Porto 3-1 AS Roma (agg: 4-3)
Bayern Munich 1-3 Liverpool (agg: 1-3)
Manchester City 7-0 Schalke (agg: 10-2)
Juventus 3-0 Atletico Madrid (agg: 3-2)
Barcelona 5-1 Lyon (agg: 5-1)

Quarter-final 1st leg

Liverpool 2-0 Porto
Tottenham Hotspur 1-0 Manchester City
Ajax 1-1 Juventus
Manchester United 0-1 Barcelona

Quarter-final 2nd leg

Barcelona 3-0 Manchester United (agg: 4-0)
Juventus 1-2 Ajax (agg: 2-3)
Manchester City 4-3 Tottenham Hotspur (agg: 4-4, Tottenham win on away goals)
Porto 1-4 Liverpool (agg: 1-6)

Semi-final 1st leg

Tottenham Hotspur 0-1 Ajax
Barcelona 3-0 Liverpool

Semi-final 2nd leg

Liverpool 4-0 Barcelona (agg: 4-3)
Ajax 2-3 Tottenham Hotspur (agg: 3-3 Tottenham win on away goals)

Final

Tottenham Hotspur 0-2 Liverpool

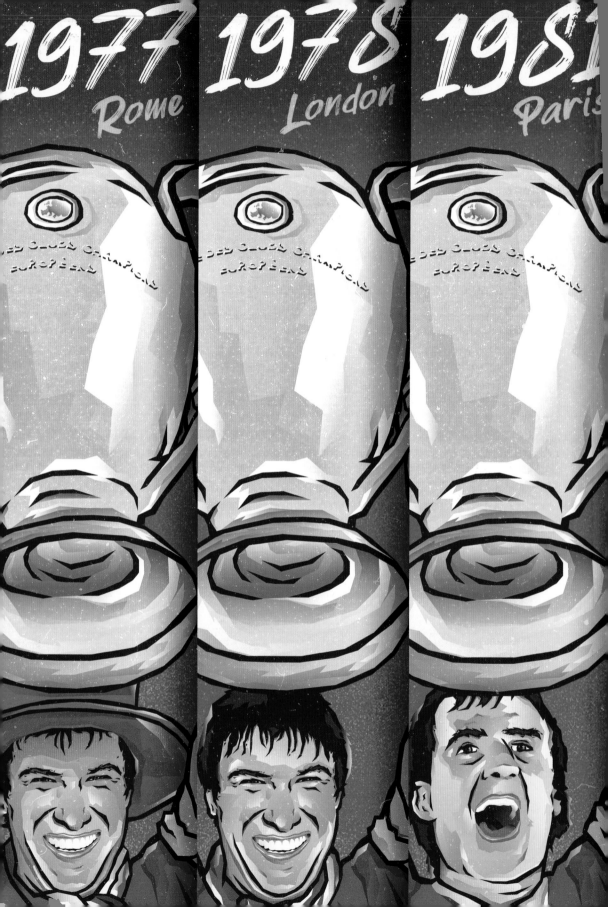